Welcome to *Contemporary Eartraining Level 1*. This book has been used by **hundreds of students** in Eartraining classes held at the former Grove School of Music in Los Angeles. As such it represents a proven and 'battle-tested' approach to the subject matter! The internationally-acclaimed Grove School provided a unique learning experience for the contemporary musician, and in this exciting environment I developed a complete Eartraining syllabus which became a vital part of the school's musicianship instruction. I am delighted to now be making my Eartraining Level 1 & 2 courses available to a wider market of students and educators! This book is self-sufficient for teachers working in private lesson or classroom settings, and for students wishing to use it as a theory/conceptual review. However, teachers as well as students working on a self-study basis will be interested to know that **cassette tapes of all the exercises in this book are available** - please see page *iv* for further information.

Some of you may be thinking, "What is Eartraining and why do I need it?" - well, it's my belief that an educated ear is the foundation we need in order to compose, arrange or perform in contemporary styles. In other words - you won't be able to write or play anything that you can't hear! A main factor distinguishing top pro musicians from the rest, is their ability to 'hear ahead' - to know what something will sound like **before** it is written or played. This of course results in greater focus and accuracy in the musical end product. Also the ability to hear what other performers are doing, either live or transcribing from recordings, is a vital goal for a great many musicians! The bottom line is that **the mastery of Eartraining skills will enable you to achieve these goals!**

My Eartraining books & courses use a key-center based 'relative pitch' method. By this I mean that the ear first needs to identify where the tonic or 'home-base' of a given key is, and then to establish the 'active-to-resting' resolutions that occur within the key. There are two vital consequences to this approach - firstly it empowers you to discard bad habits like 'singing up the scale' to find out where you are, and secondly you will be identifying the 'resolutions' in every key in exactly the same manner. In order to do this, we need a method of labelling the scale degrees which will apply to all keys - my books use the '**SOLFEG**' (short for 'solfeggio') system. This simply entails calling the major scale degrees by their 'solfeg' names - **DO, RE, MI, FA, SO, LA, TI** and back to **DO**. Famous 'solfeg' users include Julie Andrews in the Sound of Music!! The beauty of using this system is that '**DO**' can be assigned to **any key** - the scale resolutions will work in exactly the same manner! Indeed I believe that it is vital for the modern musician to be able to hear melody and harmony in the same way regardless of the actual key used - hence the problems with the so-called eartraining methods advocating 'perfect pitch' that I sometimes see advertised. The **SOLFEG** syllables and associated 'active & resting' qualities within the major scale, are reviewed for you in Chapter 1, page 7.

Here in *Contemporary Eartraining Level 1* we will work on hearing and transcribing major scale resolutions and melodies, melodic and harmonic intervals, diatonic triads and bass lines. All intervals occurring within the scale are progressively studied and recognized during the course, both melodically (one note following another) and harmonically (two notes sounding simultaneously). Diatonic (meaning 'belonging to a key') triads are first studied and recognized individually, and then combined in short progressions and used to harmonize simple melodies. Bass lines are introduced as melodies in the bass register, and also studied from harmonic and root interval standpoints. Throughout the book, we are progressively working with different rhythms, beginning with whole, half and quarter notes (see Chapter 1 page 6) and gradually introducing eighth-note rhythmic figures and anticipations.

The book is divided into eight chapters, which are designed to be studied 'in sequence' and which progressively introduce and develop the areas outlined above. This organization is appropriate for classroom situations as well as private study. At the Grove School, we were running ten-week quarterly semesters, and in the class I would cover the first four chapters prior to a mid-term test, and the remaining four chapters prior to a final test. The material can also be adapted for use within different length semesters/courses, at the discretion of the teacher. The cassette tapes available with the book contain practice material and homework assignments for each chapter.

Each chapter in this book consists of the following sections:-
- explanation & illustration of the new music concepts presented in the chapter
- summary of classroom and/or study activities required to learn the concepts
- vocal drills (using SOLFEG syllables) and melodies, for practice purposes
- summary of theory and eartraining assignments for the chapter
- workbook questions (which can be filled out) and answers for verification.

Note to teachers - when using this book in private or group class situations, you can play from the 'Workbook Answers' section of each chapter when drilling your students - they can then fill out their answers in the corresponding 'Workbook Questions' section. For students wishing to drill the material on a self-study basis, you can listen to the cassette tapes which are available (see page *iv*) when filling out the Workbook Questions - this can be verified against the Workbook Answers. (Also, teachers using this material may feel that it is productive for the students to be using the tapes between classes - this is certainly true in my own experience)!

Working on the melodic, harmonic and rhythmic concepts in this book is the perfect preparation for my *Contemporary Eartraining Level 2* course, which deals extensively with hearing 3- and 4-part chord progressions, as well as melodies across key changes and modal scales. Good luck with Eartraining - and I hope it opens many doors for you as a musician!!

Mark Harrison
Harrison Music Education Systems
Los Angeles, California

MARK HARRISON has been active as a keyboardist, composer and arranger for over twenty years. Before moving to Los Angeles in 1987, his musical career in his native London included extensive club and studio experience as well as appearances on British national (**BBC**) television. In 1985 Mark began his association with **De Wolfe Ltd.**, a leading international music publisher with the world's largest recorded music 'library'. To date Mark has written, arranged and recorded five albums for this company, in a wide variety of contemporary styles. Mark's music has been used by such clients as **American Express**, **CNN**, **Ford Motor Company**, **True Value Hardware**, **Harris & Frank**, **The New Hair Institute** and many others - including the **British Labor Party** who chose one of Mark's tunes as a recurrent 'theme' in political broadcasts during a national election!

Since moving to the USA, Mark has immersed himself in the music scene in Los Angeles. In recent years his activities have included playing keyboards and writing for various Los Angeles-based rock and fusion bands (featuring some top studio musicians) as well as a number of writing/recording collaborations in styles ranging from pop to jazz to new age music. In 1988 Mark began teaching at the **Grove School of Music** in Los Angeles, an internationally acclaimed contemporary music institution with students from all around the world. Mark's education commitments at the school quickly grew to include the teaching of contemporary keyboard styles, pop arranging, playing ensembles, harmony/theory and eartraining classes. He wrote numerous courses and music textbooks which became an integral part of the Grove School curriculum, prompting the **American Federation of Musicians** to observe that he had "enriched the musical community of Los Angeles".

Mark is the founder of the **HARRISON SCHOOL OF MUSIC** (a successor institution to the original Grove School) in Los Angeles, California - see page *vi* for further information! His keyboard method "**The Pop Piano Book**" has received critical acclaim from top professional musicians and educators alike, and the music education books and tapes marketed by **Harrison Music Education Systems** are now sold all around the world. In August of 1994 the **Berklee College of Music** began stocking all of Mark's music education methods. Apart from his work in the education field, Mark's other recent projects have included the composing and sequencing of music for **Roland** and **Gibson** products shows and for a series on the **Arts & Entertainment** TV network, as well as showcases, arranging work and album sessions for a diverse mixture of contemporary pop artists. Mark's energy, clarity and passion for conveying the wonders of music through his books, in the classroom and in his private tutoring, combine to make him a uniquely effective contemporary music educator.

The ***CONTEMPORARY EARTRAINING LEVEL ONE BOOK*** contains hundreds of music drills and exercises.

If you are a **student** who would like to work through this material on a self-study basis, or if you are a **teacher** who feels that this self-study option would be of value to your students, you'll be interested to know that all these exercises are available ***RECORDED ON TAPE*** - (a total of nearly five hours of material on four cassette tapes).

If you would like to order these tapes, please call toll-free (in the U.S.):-

1-800-799-HMES

(**H**arrison **M**usic **E**ducation **S**ystems)

or you may write to us at:-

HARRISON MUSIC EDUCATION SYSTEMS
P.O. BOX 56505
SHERMAN OAKS
CA 91413 USA

Here are some other books available from

HARRISON MUSIC EDUCATION SYSTEMS:-

Contemporary Eartraining Level Two

- a modern approach to help you hear and transcribe chord progressions, modal scales, and 'II-V-I' style modulations and melodies (available with three cassette tapes of exercises). Developed at the **Grove School of Music** in Los Angeles.

The Pop Piano Book

- a complete ground-up method for playing contemporary styles spontaneously on the keyboard. This 500-page book includes review of harmonic and rhythmic concepts, application of harmony to the keyboard in all keys, and then specific instruction for playing in pop, rock, funk, country, ballad, new age and gospel styles. This unique book is endorsed by **Grammy-winners** and top educators, and is available with cassette tapes and MIDI files of all 800 music examples!

...and we're working on the following books for Fall '95 release...

Contemporary Music Theory Level One

- this introductory theory course covers music notation, key signatures, basic scales, intervals, modes, diatonic relationships and three- & four-part chords. Includes hundreds of written theory exercises with answers!

Contemporary Music Theory Level Two

- this intermediate theory course covers larger chord forms and more complex scales, 'definitive' chords in major and minor keys, analysis of key centers in tunes, 'upper structure' voicings, modal harmonization and voiceleading. Includes hundreds of written theory exercises with answers!

Your product inquiries are welcome - please see previous page for contact information!

- *The HARRISON SCHOOL OF MUSIC (based in Los Angeles, California) is running group Eartraining classes using our unique CONTEMPORARY EARTRAINING method books!*

- *The school also offers Keyboard and Music Theory classes based on the acclaimed musicianship methods from HARRISON MUSIC EDUCATION SYSTEMS (see page v), as well as classes in voice, guitar and recording.*

- *School founder MARK HARRISON was on the faculty at the internationally-acclaimed GROVE SCHOOL OF MUSIC for several years. The success of the Grove School proved that there was a need for in-depth pop & jazz education taught by working professionals - this is now being provided in the Los Angeles area by the HARRISON SCHOOL OF MUSIC!*

If you would like more information on the school, or would like to inquire about private instruction with MARK HARRISON, please call toll-free (in the U.S.):-

1-800-828-MUSIC

or you may write to us at:-

HARRISON SCHOOL OF MUSIC
P.O. BOX 56505
SHERMAN OAKS
CA 91413 USA

I would like to take this opportunity to thank all of my fellow musicians and educators for their influence, and also the many friends and students who over the years have used this book and given me valuable comments and feedback. You are encouraged to do the same - write to me at P.O. Box 56505, Sherman Oaks, CA 91413 when you have the chance!

In addition, the following people deserve an honourable mention for their important contributions to this book:-

Dick Grove — Dick spent a considerable amount of time doing the initial data entry and preparation of my Eartraining books on the computer, and of course he created the unique educational environment at the Grove School within which I was able to develop my music education materials.

Dan Friedman — Dan provided important technical assistance in the subsequent recapturing and conversion of the computer files for this book, prior to it being edited and re-issued.

Guy Harrison — no relation! Guy deserves a special thank-you for his considerable help in the digital re-mastering of the Eartraining tapes.

Thanks guys!!

Contemporary Eartraining Level 1 by Mark Harrison

1. *Introduction*

1.1.   This eight-chapter course functions as a first-level eartraining method. We will start out by reviewing major scale melodic resolutions (using the 'SOLFEG' system) and some music theory & notation basics. We will then begin the study of interval relationships to encompass all melodic and harmonic intervals occurring within a major scale. These resolutions and intervals will form the basis of melodic dictation exercises. We will also reinforce these concepts by various vocal drills using 'SOLFEG'. Diatonic triads will also be identified and used to harmonize melodies.

1.2.   As we progressively work through the various intervals and melody combinations we will continue to develop our rhythmic notation and recognition skills in a graduated fashion. Initially the drills and transcription exercises will be in the keys of C, F and G, and will then progressively include other keys during the later part of the course. Bass line dictation and diatonic chord progressions will also be addressed at this point, which then serves as an introduction to hearing the harmonic concepts presented in ***Contemporary Eartraining Level 2***.

Review of major scales, resolutions and SOLFEG

1.   *Theory and Notation Basics*

1.1.   First of all we need to review some theory concepts relating to key signatures and solfeg syllables. Let's consider the following major scale examples:

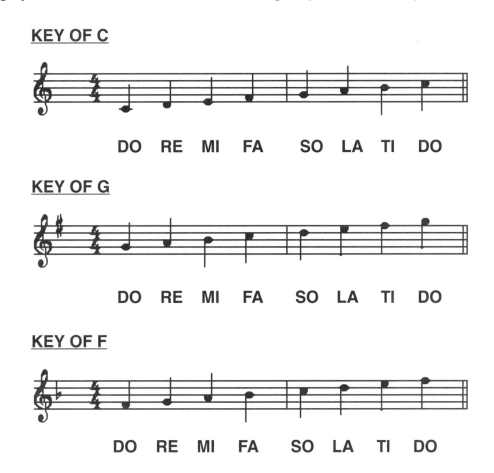

KEY OF C

DO   RE   MI   FA   SO   LA   TI   DO

KEY OF G

DO   RE   MI   FA   SO   LA   TI   DO

KEY OF F

DO   RE   MI   FA   SO   LA   TI   DO

1.2.   Note the key signatures for C major (no sharps or flats), G major (one sharp) and F major (one flat) respectively.

1.3.   The 'solfeg' syllables are used to represent the scale degrees of a major scale or 'key center'. Note that in the above examples 'DO' has been re-assigned in each case to the key required. We are always trying to hear melody and harmony in relation to 'DO' or the tonal center, regardless of the actual pitch 'DO' happens to be in any given piece of music.

1.4.   In this first chapter we we will be working with the following rhythmic subdivisions or 'permutations' within a measure:-

a) <u>WHOLE NOTE</u> (4 beats)

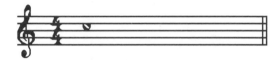

b) <u>HALF NOTE/HALF NOTE</u> (2 beats each)

c) <u>DOTTED HALF NOTE</u> (3 beats)/**<u>QUARTER NOTE</u>** (1 beat)

d) <u>HALF NOTE</u> (2 beats)/**<u>QUARTER NOTE/QUARTER NOTE</u>** (1 beat each)

e) <u>QUARTER NOTE/QUARTER NOTE</u> (1 beat each)/**<u>HALF NOTE</u>** (2 beats)

f) <u>FOUR QUARTER NOTES</u> (1 beat each)

In **4/4** time beats 1 and 3 can be thought of as the 'primary beats' or strong beats. All the above rhythms can be considered in terms of their relationship to the primary beats of the measure. Notice that in all cases the total number of beats in each measure adds up to the time signature i.e. 4 beats.

2.   *Major scale active/resting and resolution concepts*

2.1.   When using the SOLFEG system, each major scale degree implies an active or resting quality. Here again for your reference are the solfeg syllables applied to a C major scale:-

DO RE MI FA   SO LA TI   DO

These 'active or resting' attributes can be summarized as follows:-

DO - Always the most resting or 'resolved' tone within the major scale.

RE - This is an active tone which would like to resolve down to **DO** (or up to **MI**). Technically we would call **RE** an 'active whole-step' as it is a whole-step away from adjacent resting tones (**DO** and **MI**).

MI - **MI**, like **DO**, is also a resting or 'resolved' tone within the major scale.

FA - This is an active tone which would like to resolve down to **MI**. Technically we would call **FA** an 'active half-step' as it is a half step away from the resting tone **MI**.

SO - **SO**, like **DO** and **MI**, is a resting or 'resolved' tone within the major scale.

LA - This is an active tone which would like to resolve down to **SO** (or up to **DO** via **TI**). Technically we would call **LA** on 'active whole-step' as it is a whole-step away from the resting tone **SO**.

TI - This is an active tone which would like to resolve up to **DO**. Technically we would call **TI** an 'active half-step' as it is a half-step away from the resting tone **DO**.

2.2.   We will also see that the most common (naturally-occurring) resolutions between active and resting scale degrees are **RE to DO**, **FA to MI**, **LA to SO**, and **TI to DO**. In the keys of C, G, and F, these are notated as follows:-

2.2. contd.

KEY OF C

Remember that the goal is to hear and recognize all of the active-to-resting resolutions in exactly the same way regardless of the key i.e. **FA** to **MI** in F major should sound the same as **FA** to **MI** in C major! In each case the ear is hearing a resolution with respect to **DO**.

3. Class/Study Activities

3.1. Resolution and pitch singing/recognition

(**N.B.** 'DO' or the tonic of the key, is always given as a reference tone before each drill).
- Singing and recognizing **RE-DO**, **FA-MI**, **LA-SO** and **TI-DO** resolutions, in the keys of C, G and F
- Individual pitch recognition in DO-DO (1 octave) range, in the keys of C, G, F (the goal is to hear each pitch as the active or resting component of a resolution)

3.2. Melodic dictation/transcription

- Transcribing melodies in DO-DO (1 octave) range using rhythmic values in **1.4.**, in the keys of C, G and F (again listen for active & resting tones in the melodies).

(3.1.)   **VOCAL DRILLS - RESOLUTIONS - KEY OF C**

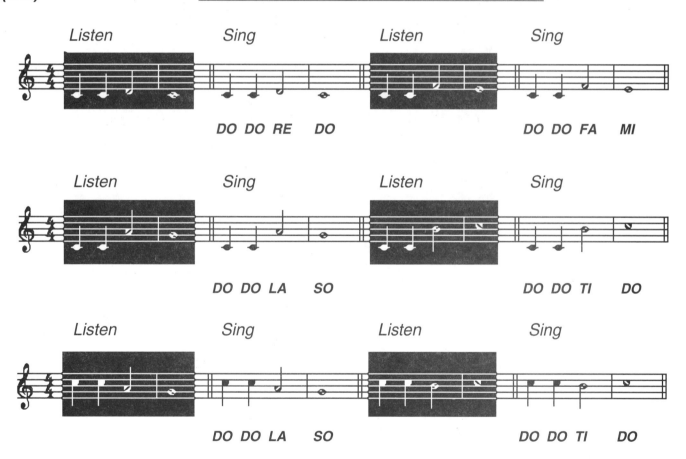

(3.1. Contd) <u>VOCAL DRILLS - RESOLUTIONS - KEY OF G</u>

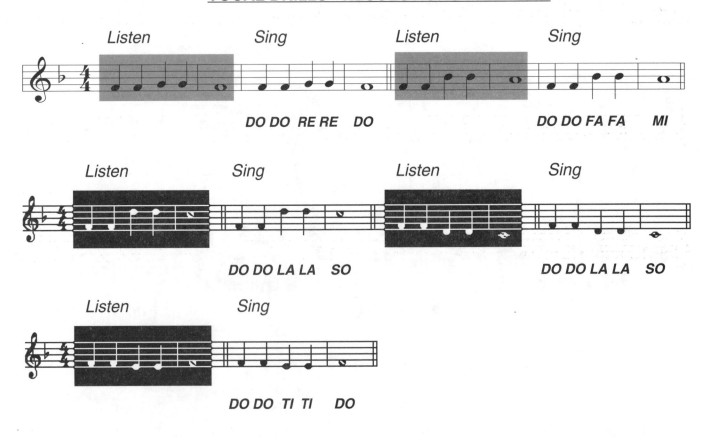

DO DO RE DO   DO DO FA MI

DO DO LA SO   DO DO TI DO

DO DO FA MI

<u>VOCAL DRILLS - RESOLUTIONS - KEY OF F</u>

DO DO RE RE DO   DO DO FA FA MI

DO DO LA LA SO   DO DO LA LA SO

DO DO TI TI DO

(3.2.)   **<u>MELODIES FOR SINGING AND TRANSCRIPTION</u>**

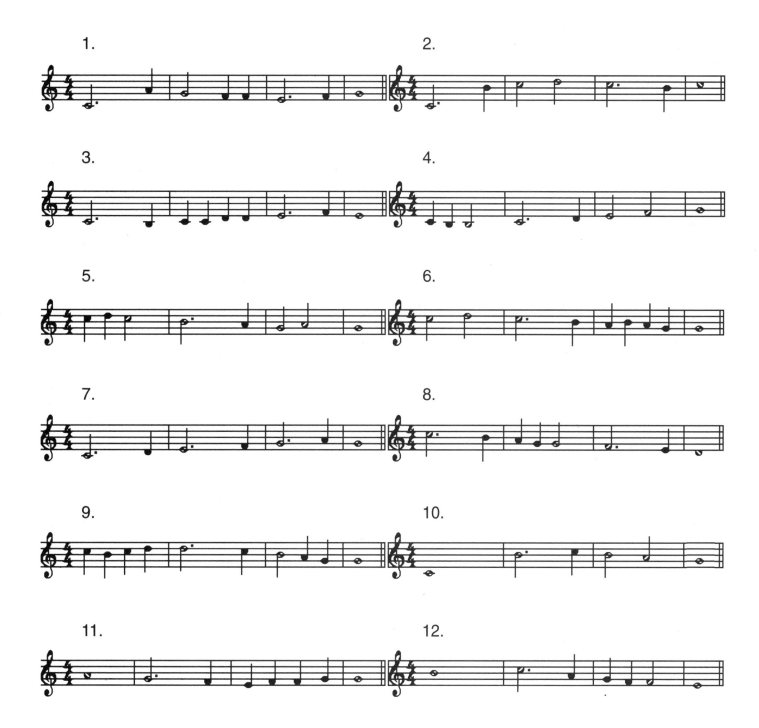

(3.2. contd)   <u>**MELODIES FOR SINGING AND TRANSCRIPTION (contd)**</u>

13. 14.

15. 16.

17. 18.

19. 20.

<u>**4.**</u>   <u>**Theory Assignments**</u>

4.1.   **Supplementary Worksheet - Keys of C** *(p193),* **G** *(p199)* **and F** *(p205).*

-      Write out notes on the treble clef staff corresponding to the resolutions RE-DO, FA-MI, LA-SO and TI-DO.

<u>**5.**</u>   <u>**Eartraining Tapes Available** *(see page iv)* **- tape contents for this chapter**</u>

5.1.   **The Eartraining tape available for Chapter 1 consists of the following:-**

-      copies of the resolution singing drills (see **3.1.**) for practice purposes
-      resolution and pitch identification questions
    -      you may fill out your answers in sections **6.1.** and **6.2.**
    -      you may check against correct answers in sections **7.1.** and **7.2.**
-      melodic dictation/transcription questions
    -      you may fill out your answers in section **6.3.**
    -      you may check against correct answers in section **7.3.**

6.   Eartraining Assignments - Workbook Questions

Note to students - *if you are doing the Eartraining Assignments, the Workbook Questions section in each chapter is where you write your answers. If you are studying with an instructor, they can use the corresponding Workbook Answers section as a source of questions - otherwise you can do the Assignments on a self-study basis using the cassette tapes which are available (see page iv). Don't forget that 'solfeg' works in all keys - so for the resolution and pitch questions (6.1. & 6.2.) requiring solfeg syllable answers, the actual key used is not important providing you can relate to the DO used in each case!*

Note to teachers - *if you are drilling students on this material, you can play from the corresponding Workbook Answers section, and the students can fill out their answers here.*

6.1.   Resolution Identification

These 16 questions consist of either **RE-DO**, **FA-MI**, **LA-SO** or **TI-DO** resolutions. You are to identify which resolution is being played. Write your answers (solfeg) below:

1.	___ ___		9.	___ ___
2.	___ ___		10.	___ ___
3.	___ ___		11.	___ ___
4.	___ ___		12.	___ ___
5.	___ ___		13.	___ ___
6.	___ ___		14.	___ ___
7.	___ ___		15.	___ ___
8.	___ ___		16.	___ ___

6.2.   Pitch Identification

You are to identify which pitch is being played (in DO - DO 1 octave range). Each pitch is either the active or resting component of a resolution. Write your answers (solfeg) below:-

1.	___		9.	___
2.	___		10.	___
3.	___		11.	___
4.	___		12.	___
5.	___		13.	___
6.	___		14.	___
7.	___		15.	___
8.	___		16.	___

6.3.   Melodic Dictation/Transcription

These melodies are based upon the examples used in this chapter. Note from the key signatures that the keys of C, G and F are being used. Write your answers on the following page (again don't forget to listen for the *active & resting qualities* and *resolutions* present):-

13

6.3. contd.   **MELODIC DICTATION/TRANSCRIPTION**

1.

2.

3.

4.

5.

6.

7.

8.

9.

10.

7.   Eartraining Assignments - Workbook Answers

Note to students - if you are doing the Eartraining Assignments, the Workbook Answers section in each chapter is where you check your answers. If you are studying with an instructor, they can use this section as a source of questions to drill you on the material - otherwise you can use this section to verify your work if you are doing the Assignments on a self-study basis using the cassette tapes which are available (see page **iv**).

Note to teachers - if you are drilling students on this material, you can play from the Workbook Answers section in each chapter, and the students can fill out their answers in the corresponding Workbook Questions section. Be sure to play **DO** as a reference before each question! In the questions requiring solfeg answers (i.e. the resolutions and pitches on this page) the actual key used is not important - however students may feel more reassured if you stay with the key of C to begin with.

7.1.   Resolution Identification answers

I.	FA	-	MI	9.	RE	-	DO
2.	RE	-	DO	10.	TI	-	DO
3.	LA	-	SO	11.	LA	-	SO
4.	TI	-	DO	12.	FA	-	MI
5.	FA	-	MI	13.	LA	-	SO
6.	RE	-	DO	14.	RE	-	DO
7.	LA	-	SO	15.	FA	-	MI
8.	TI	-	DO	16.	TI	-	DO

7.2.   Pitch Identification answers

1.	MI	9.	MI
2.	RE	10.	RE
3.	FA	11.	FA
4.	TI	12.	LA
5.	SO	13.	SO
6.	LA	14.	FA
7.	TI	15.	TI
8.	FA	16.	RE

7.3. MELODIC DICTATION/TRANSCRIPTION ANSWERS

Major 3rd/Minor 6th intervals and 8th-note rhythms

1.   *Theory and Notation*

1.1.   We will now begin to consider the interval relationships found within a major scale. The first intervals we will consider are the major 3rd and minor 6th intervals. The major 3rd has a span of 2 whole-steps. The minor 6th has a span of 4 whole steps and is the inversion of the major 3rd interval.

1.2.   These are the melodic major 3rd and minor 6th intervals present within the major scale:-

KEY OF C

Melodic Major 3rds ascending

DO   MI   FA   LA   (SO)   SO   TI   (DO)

Melodic Major 3rds descending

MI   DO   LA   FA   (MI)   TI   SO

Melodic Minor 6ths ascending

MI   DO   LA   FA   (MI)   TI   SO

Melodic Minor 6ths descending

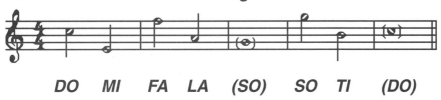

DO   MI   FA   LA   (SO)   SO   TI   (DO)

1.2. contd.

KEY OF G

Melodic Major 3rds ascending

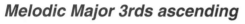

DO   MI   FA   LA   (SO)   SO   TI   (DO)

Melodic Major 3rds descending

MI   DO   LA   FA   (MI)   TI   SO

Melodic Minor 6ths ascending

MI   DO   LA   FA   (MI)   TI   SO

Melodic Minor 6ths descending

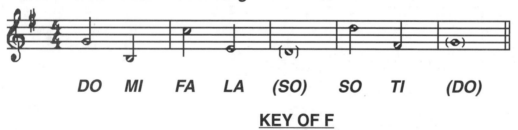

DO   MI   FA   LA   (SO)   SO   TI   (DO)

KEY OF F

Melodic Major 3rds ascending

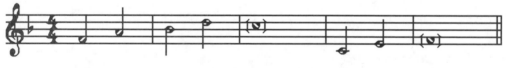

DO   MI   FA   LA   (SO)   SO   TI   (DO)

Melodic Major 3rds descending

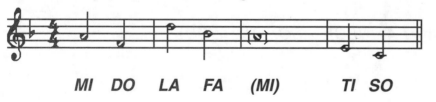

MI   DO   LA   FA   (MI)   TI   SO

1.2. contd.

KEY OF F Continued

Melodic Minor 6ths ascending

MI	DO	LA	FA	(MI)	TI	SO

Melodic Minor 6ths descending

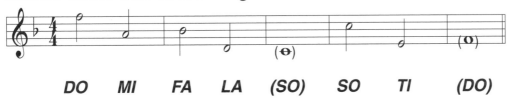

DO	MI	FA	LA	(SO)	SO	TI	(DO)

Note that when an interval ends on an active tone, the natural resolution from the active tone to the appropriate resting tone is also shown i.e. FA-LA to SO.

1.3. These are the harmonic major 3rds and minor 6th intervals present within the major scale:-

KEY OF C

Harmonic Major 3rds

MI	LA	TI
DO	FA	SO

Harmonic Minor 6ths

DO	FA	SO
MI	LA	TI

19

1.3. contd.

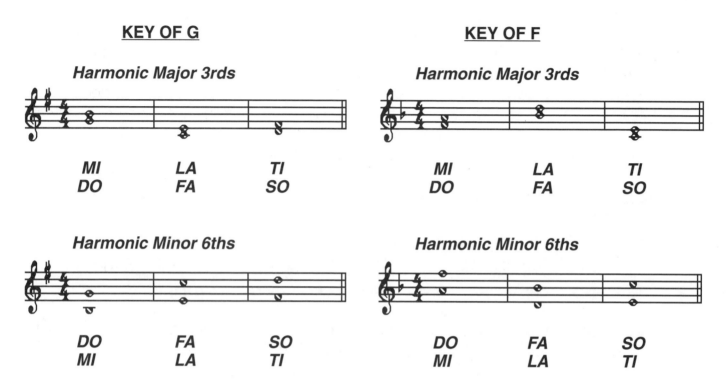

KEY OF G	KEY OF F

Harmonic Major 3rds

MI   LA   TI
DO   FA   SO

Harmonic Major 3rds

MI   LA   TI
DO   FA   SO

Harmonic Minor 6ths

DO   FA   SO
MI   LA   TI

Harmonic Minor 6ths

DO   FA   SO
MI   LA   TI

1.4.   Major 3rd and minor 6th intervals will have a strong and melodic character. The larger span of the 6th will additionally result in a 'broad' impression. When heard harmonically these intervals will have a warm and consonant sound. The 3rd could be considered as adjacent tones of a triad, while the 6th could be considered as the outer tones of an inverted triad.

1.5.   All major 3rd and minor 6th intervals will consist of either DO-MI, FA-LA or SO-TI 'pairs' of notes. In addition to the above-mentioned interval characteristics, there will also be differences in impression due to the respective active/resting qualities.

DO-MI/ MI-DO	Always the most resting or stable major 3rd/minor 6th interval. Both of these tones are resting tones.
FA-LA/ LA-FA	Both of these tones are active, creating an active interval. Melodically when ending on **FA** (ascending minor 6th/descending major 3rd) the interval will want to resolve to **MI**. When ending on **LA** (ascending major 3rd/descending minor 6th) the interval will want to resolve to **SO**.

1.5. contd.

SO-TI/   **SO** is a resting tone and **TI** is an active tone. Melodically when ending on
TI-SO   TI (ascending major 3rd/descending minor 6th) the interval will want to
resolve to **DO**. When ending on **SO** (ascending minor 6th/descending
major 3rd) the interval will not need resolution as we have landed on the
resting tone **SO**. However, this is something of an 'unprepared' resolution
as we have not resolved into **SO** via an adjacent active tone.

1.6.   Also in this chapter we will discuss some new rhythmic combinations featuring
pairs of eighth notes. The eighth note has a rhythmic value of one-half of a beat. When written
in pairs they will be 'beamed' together as in the following examples:

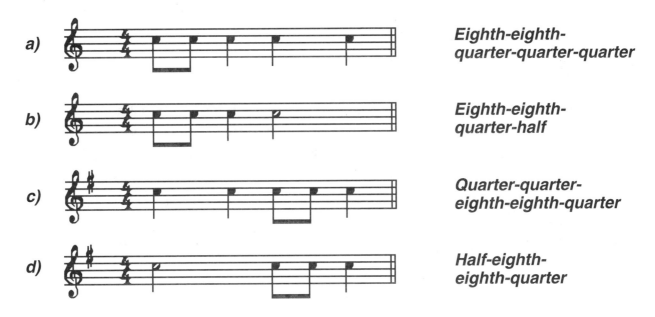

a)   *Eighth-eighth-quarter-quarter-quarter*

b)   *Eighth-eighth-quarter-half*

c)   *Quarter-quarter-eighth-eighth-quarter*

d)   *Half-eighth-eighth-quarter*

1.7.   In a melodic context these rhythmic patterns might occur as follows:-

KEY OF C

DO RE MI FA   MI

SO LA SO DO

1.7. contd.

KEY OF G

TI   *DO*   *DO*   *RE*   *MI*

KEY OF F

FA   *MI*   *RE*   *DO*

1.8.   Notice that the total number of beats in each measure still adds up to the time signature (i.e. 4 beats). Again we can still hear the primary beats (i.e. on 1 and 3) in the above examples, and hearing these 'guideposts' is useful when learning the rhythmic phrases.

2.   *Class/Study Activities*

2.1.   *Pitch singing and recognition*

-     Individual pitch recognition in DO - DO (1 octave) range, in the keys of C, G & F

2.2.   *Interval singing and recognition*

-     Singing drills using major 3rd and minor 6th intervals, in the keys of C, G, & F

-     Recognition of (melodic and harmonic) major 3rd and minor 6th intervals, in the keys of C, G, and F

2.3.   *Melodic dictation/transcription*

-     Transcribing melodies containing major 3rd and minor 6th intervals (using all rhythmic combinations covered so far) in the keys of C, G & F

(2.2.)

VOCAL DRILLS - MAJOR 3RD INTERVALS - KEY OF C

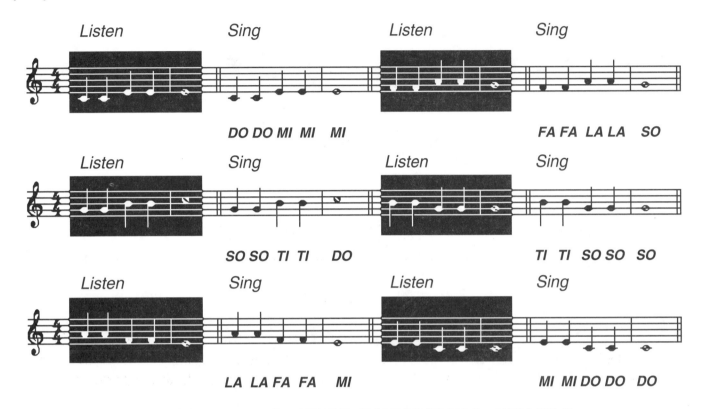

DO DO MI MI MI · FA FA LA LA SO

SO SO TI TI DO · TI TI SO SO SO

LA LA FA FA MI · MI MI DO DO DO

VOCAL DRILLS - MINOR 6TH INTERVALS - KEY OF C

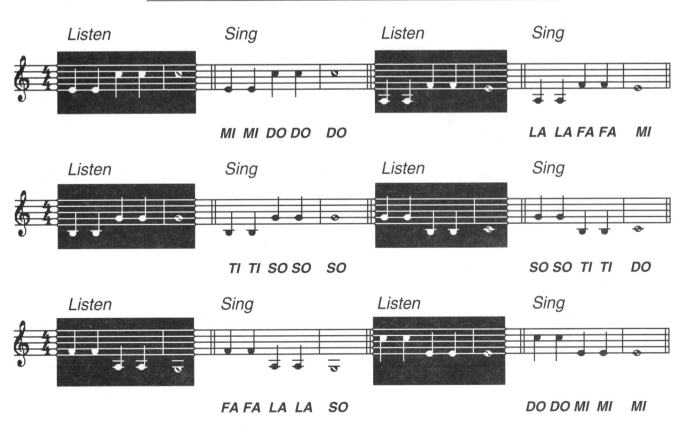

MI MI DO DO DO · LA LA FA FA MI

TI TI SO SO SO · SO SO TI TI DO

FA FA LA LA SO · DO DO MI MI MI

(2.2. contd.) <u>VOCAL DRILLS - MAJOR 3RD INTERVALS - KEY OF G</u>

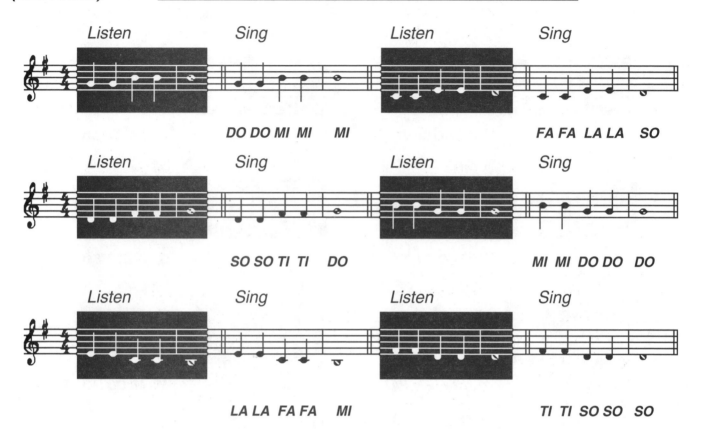

DO DO MI MI   MI

FA FA LA LA   SO

SO SO TI TI   DO

MI MI DO DO   DO

LA LA FA FA   MI

TI TI SO SO   SO

<u>VOCAL DRILLS - MINOR 6TH INTERVALS - KEY OF G</u>

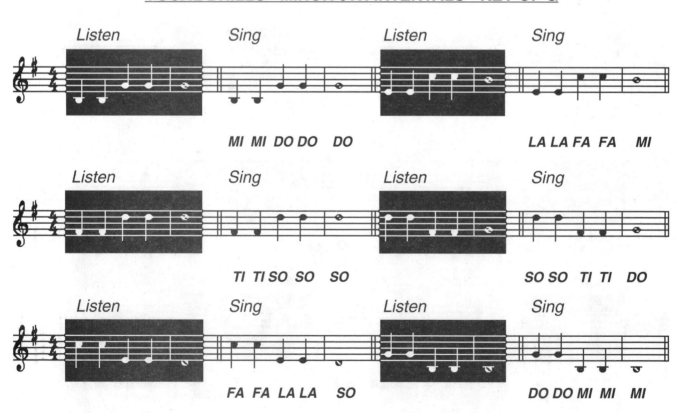

MI MI DO DO   DO

LA LA FA FA   MI

TI TI SO SO   SO

SO SO TI TI   DO

FA FA LA LA   SO

DO DO MI MI   MI

(2.2. contd.) **VOCAL DRILLS - MAJOR 3RD INTERVALS - KEY OF F**

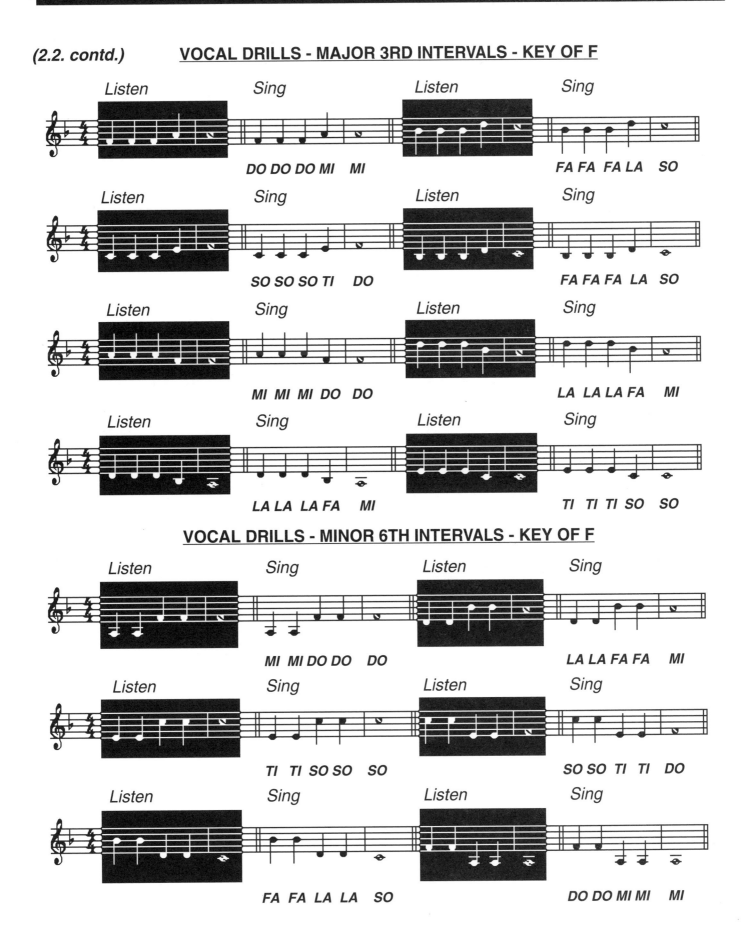

VOCAL DRILLS - MINOR 6TH INTERVALS - KEY OF F

(2.3.)   **MELODIES FOR SINGING AND TRANSCRIPTION**

(2.3. contd.) <u>**MELODIES FOR SINGING AND TRANSCRIPTION (contd)**</u>

3. Theory Assignments

3.1. Supplementary Worksheet - Keys of C (p193), G (p199) and F (p205).

- Write out the notes on the treble clef staff corresponding to the major 3rd and minor 6th intervals (ascending and descending) followed by the appropriate resolutions for intervals ending on active tones (review **1.2.** as required).

4. Eartraining Tapes Available (see page iv) - tape contents for this chapter

4.1. The Eartraining tape available for Chapter 2 consists of the following:-

- copies of the major 3rd and minor 6th interval drills in the keys of C, G and F (see **2.2.**) for practice purposes

- melodic interval identification questions (major 3rds/minor 6ths) ascending and descending
  - you may fill out your answers in section **5.1.**
  - you may check against correct answers in section **6.1.**

- harmonic interval identification questions (major 3rds/minor 6ths)
  - you may fill out your answers in section **5.2.**
  - you may check against correct answers in section **6.2.**

- melodic dictation/transcription questions
  - you may fill out your answers in section **5.3.**
  - you may check against correct answers in section **6.3.**

5.   *Eartraining Assignments - Workbook Questions*

This is the section where you fill out your answers. Note that the melodic and harmonic interval questions in this book **will be presented in different keys** i.e. here in Chapter 2 they begin in **C** major before moving to **F** and **G**. In each case however you are given DO (the tonic of the key) as a reference, and the goal is to hear the solfeg relationship (i.e. active and/or resting qualities) of the interval with respect to DO, **regardless of the actual key being used**.

5.1.   *Melodic Interval Identification*

Questions 1 - 10 consist of Major 3rd intervals ascending or descending. The options are **DO-MI** (ascending), **MI-DO** (descending), **FA-LA** (ascending), **LA-FA** (descending), **SO-TI** (ascending) or **TI-SO** (descending). Write your (solfeg) answers below:-

1.   _____ _____   6.   _____ _____
2.   _____ _____   7.   _____ _____
3.   _____ _____   8.   _____ _____
4.   _____ _____   9.   _____ _____
5.   _____ _____   10. _____ _____

Questions 11 - 20 consist of Minor 6th intervals ascending or descending. The options are **MI-DO** (ascending), **DO-MI** (descending), **LA-FA** (ascending), **FA-LA** (descending), **TI-SO** (ascending) or **SO-TI** (descending). Write your (solfeg) answers below:-

11. _____ _____   16. _____ _____
12. _____ _____   17. _____ _____
13. _____ _____   18. _____ _____
14. _____ _____   19. _____ _____
15. _____ _____   20. _____ _____

Questions 21-36 now comprise all of the above interval possibilities (i.e. Major 3rds and Minor 6ths, ascending and descending). For each question, write the solfeg that you hear, and the interval description (either **Ma3** or **Mi6**) in parentheses.

21. _____ _____ (   )   29. _____ _____ (   )
22. _____ _____ (   )   30. _____ _____ (   )
23. _____ _____ (   )   31. _____ _____ (   )
24. _____ _____ (   )   32. _____ _____ (   )
25. _____ _____ (   )   33. _____ _____ (   )
26. _____ _____ (   )   34. _____ _____ (   )
27. _____ _____ (   )   35. _____ _____ (   )
28. _____ _____ (   )   36. _____ _____ (   )

5.2.   *Harmonic Interval Identification*

Questions 1-6 consist of Major 3rd intervals played harmonically i.e. both tones played simultaneously. The options are **DO-MI**, **FA-LA** or **SO-TI**. Write your (solfeg) answers below:-

1.   ____ ____   4.   ____ ____

2.   ____ ____   5.   ____ ____

3.   ____ ____   6.   ____ ____

Questions 7-12 consist of Minor 6th intervals played harmonically i.e. both tones played simultaneously. The options are **MI-DO**, **LA-FA** or **TI-SO**. Write your (solfeg) answers below:-

7.   ____ ____   10.   ____ ____

8.   ____ ____   11.   ____ ____

9.   ____ ____   12.   ____ ____

Questions 13-24 now comprise all the above possibilities (i.e. harmonic Major 3rd and Minor 6th intervals). For each question, write the solfeg that you hear, and the interval description (either **Ma3** or **Mi6**) in parentheses:

13.   ____ ____ (   )   19.   ____ ____ (   )

14.   ____ ____ (   )   20.   ____ ____ (   )

15.   ____ ____ (   )   21.   ____ ____ (   )

16.   ____ ____ (   )   22.   ____ ____ (   )

17.   ____ ____ (   )   23.   ____ ____ (   )

18   ____ ____ (   )   24.   ____ ____ (   )

5.3.   **MELODIC DICTATION/TRANSCRIPTION**

These melodies are based upon the examples used in this chapter (see **2.5.**). _Listen for the new major 3rd and minor 6th intervals being used._ Write your answers below:-

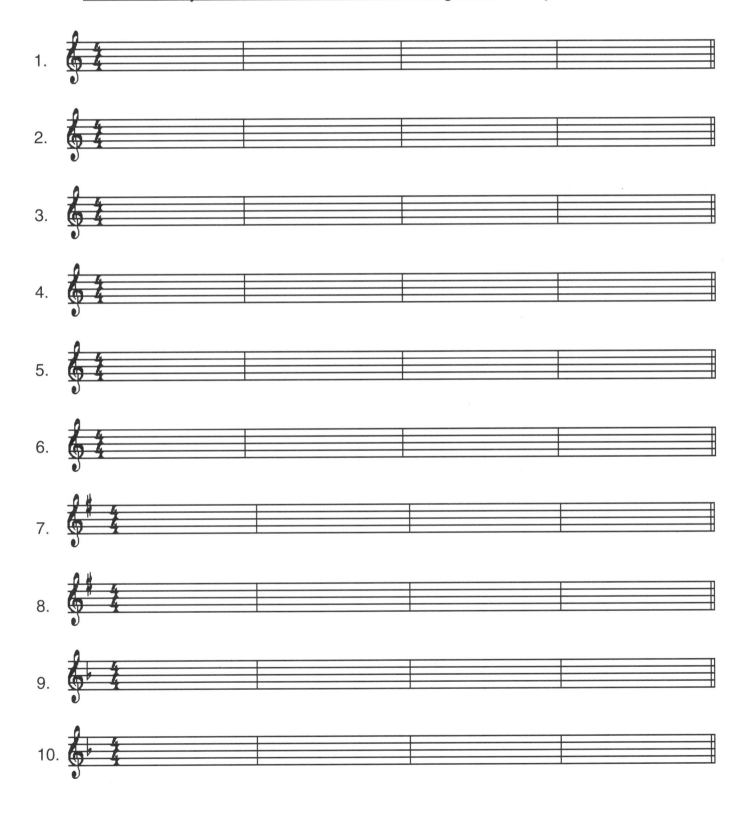

6. Eartraining Assignments - Workbook Answers

6.1. Melodic Interval Identification answers

(Major 3rds)

1.	DO	-	MI	6.	SO	-	TI
2.	LA	-	FA	7.	LA	-	FA
3.	TI	-	SO	8.	DO	-	MI
4.	FA	-	LA	9.	FA	-	LA
5.	MI	-	DO	10.	TI	-	SO

(Minor 6ths)

11.	MI	-	DO	16.	DO	-	MI
12.	TI	-	SO	17.	SO	-	TI
13.	FA	-	LA	18.	LA	-	FA
14.	DO	-	MI	19.	TI	-	SO
15.	LA	-	FA	20.	MI	-	DO

(Major 3rds/Minor 6ths)

21.	LA	-	FA	(Ma3)	29.	FA	-	LA	(Mi6)
22.	MI	-	DO	(Mi6)	30.	SO	-	TI	(Ma3)
23.	SO	-	TI	(Mi6)	31.	DO	-	MI	(Ma3)
24.	SO	-	TI	(Ma3)	32.	DO	-	MI	(Mi6)
25.	FA	-	LA	(Ma3)	33.	FA	-	LA	(Ma3)
26.	MI	-	DO	(Ma3)	34.	TI	-	SO	(Mi6)
27.	LA	-	FA	(Mi6)	35.	MI	-	DO	(Ma3)
28.	TI	-	SO	(Mi6)	36.	LA	-	FA	(Ma3)

6.2. Harmonic Interval Identification answers

(Major 3rds)

1.	DO	-	MI	4.	SO	-	TI
2.	SO	-	TI	5.	FA	-	LA
3.	FA	-	LA	6.	DO	-	MI

(Minor 6ths)

7.	LA	-	FA	10.	TI	-	SO
8.	TI	-	SO	11.	LA	-	FA
9.	MI	-	DO	12.	MI	-	DO

(Major 3rds/Minor 6ths)

13.	SO	-	TI	(Ma3)	19.	MI	-	DO	(Mi6)
14.	LA	-	FA	(Mi6)	20.	SO	-	TI	(Ma3)
15.	MI	-	DO	(Mi6)	21.	DO	-	MI	(Ma3)
16.	FA	-	LA	(Ma3)	22.	FA	-	LA	(Ma3)
17.	DO	-	MI	(Ma3)	23.	TI	-	SO	(Mi6)
18.	TI	-	SO	(Mi6)	24.	LA	-	FA	(Mi6)

6.3.   **MELODIC DICTATION/TRANSCRIPTION ANSWERS**

Minor 3rd/Major 6th intervals and I-IV-V diatonic triads

1.   Theory and Notation

1.1.   Continuing our study of the interval relationships found within a major scale, we will now focus on the diatonic minor 3rd and major 6th intervals. The minor 3rd has a span of one and a half steps (or 3 half-steps). The major 6th has a span of four and a half steps (or 9 half-steps) and is the inversion of the minor 3rd interval.

1.2.   These are the melodic minor 3rd and major 6th intervals present within the major scale:-

KEY OF C

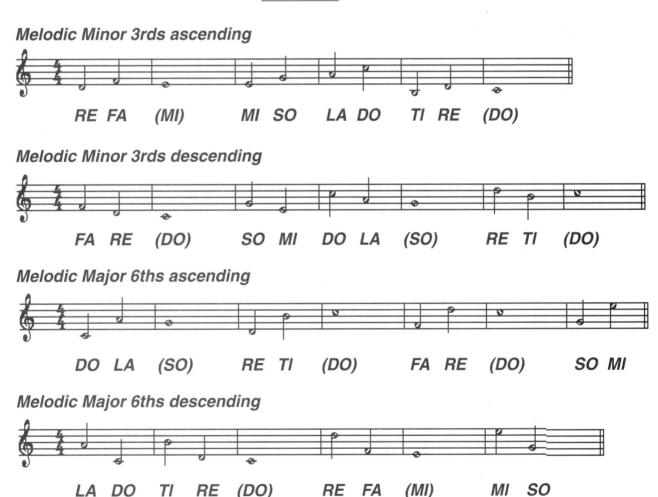

Melodic Minor 3rds ascending

RE FA (MI)   MI SO   LA DO   TI RE   (DO)

Melodic Minor 3rds descending

FA RE (DO)   SO MI   DO LA   (SO)   RE TI   (DO)

Melodic Major 6ths ascending

DO LA (SO)   RE TI (DO)   FA RE (DO)   SO MI

Melodic Major 6ths descending

LA DO TI RE (DO)   RE FA (MI)   MI SO

1.2. contd.

KEY OF G

Melodic Minor 3rds ascending

RE FA (MI)   MI SO LA DO TI RE (DO)

Melodic Minor 3rds descending

FA RE (DO)   SO MI DO LA (SO)   RE TI (DO)

Melodic Major 6ths ascending

DO LA (SO)   RE TI (DO)   FA RE (DO)   SO MI

Melodic Major 6ths descending

LA DO TI RE (DO)   RE FA (MI)   MI SO

KEY OF F

Melodic Minor 3rds ascending

RE FA (MI)   MI SO LA DO TI RE (DO)

Melodic Minor 3rds descending

FA RE (DO)   SO MI DO LA (SO)   RE TI (DO)

Melodic Major 6ths ascending

DO LA (SO)   RE TI (DO)   FA RE (DO)   SO MI

1.2. contd.   <u>KEY OF F (contd)</u>

Melodic Major 6ths descending

LA DO TI RE (DO)   RE FA (MI)   MI SO

Note that when an interval ends on an active tone, the natural resolution is also shown afterwards i.e. RE-FA resolving to MI.

1.3.   These are the harmonic minor 3rd and major 6th intervals present within the major scale:-

<u>KEY OF C</u>

Harmonic Minor 3rds

FA   SO   DO   RE
RE   MI   LA   TI

Harmonic Major 6ths

LA   TI   RE   MI
DO   RE   FA   SO

<u>KEY OF G</u>   <u>KEY OF F</u>

Harmonic Minor 3rds   ### Harmonic Minor 3rds

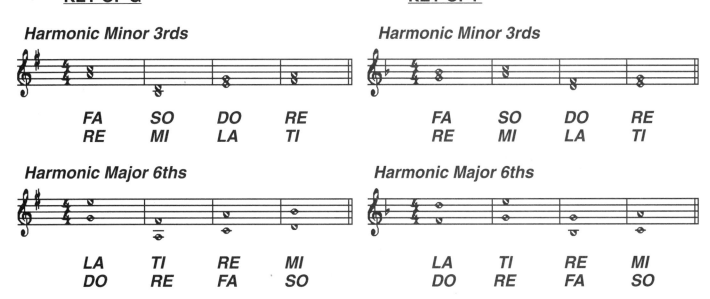

FA   SO   DO   RE   FA   SO   DO   RE
RE   MI   LA   TI   RE   MI   LA   TI

Harmonic Major 6ths   ### Harmonic Major 6ths

LA   TI   RE   MI   LA   TI   RE   MI
DO   RE   FA   SO   DO   RE   FA   SO

1.4.   The melodic interval characteristics relating to the previously discussed major 3rd and minor 6th intervals will also substantially apply to minor 3rd and major 6th intervals, i.e. they will have a strong and melodic character, with the 6th additionally having a 'broad' impression. When used harmonically these 3rds and 6ths will again sound warm and consonant - the harmonic 3rd interval can be considered as the adjacent voices of a triad, and the harmonic 6th interval can be considered as the outer voices of an inverted triad.

1.5.   All minor 3rd and major 6th intervals will consist of either RE-FA, MI-SO, LA-DO or TI-RE 'pairs' of notes. In addition to the above-mentioned interval characteristics, there will also be differences in impression due to the respective active/resting qualities:-

RE-FA/
FA-RE
Both of these tones are active, creating an active interval. Melodically when ending on **RE** (ascending major 6th/descending minor 3rd) the interval will want to resolve to **DO**. When ending on **FA** (ascending minor 3rd/descending major 6th) the interval will want to resolve to **MI**.

MI-SO/
SO-MI
Always the most resting or stable minor 3rd/major 6th interval. Both of these tones are resting tones.

LA-DO/
DO-LA
DO is a resting tone and **LA** is an active tone. Melodically when ending on **LA** (ascending major 6th/descending minor 3rd) the interval will want to resolve to **SO**. When ending on **DO** (ascending minor 3rd/descending major 6th) the interval will not need resolution as we have landed on the resting tone **DO**. However, this is something of an 'unprepared' resolution as we have not resolved into **DO** via an adjacent active tone.

TI-RE/
RE-TI
These tones are active, and create an active interval. Melodically when ending on either **RE** or **TI**, the interval will want to resolve to **DO**.

1.6.   Also in this chapter we will discuss some more rhythmic combinations featuring pairs of eighth notes. We recall from the previous chapter that the eighth note has a rhythmic value of one-half of a beat, and when eighth notes are written in pairs they are 'beamed' together as in the following examples:-

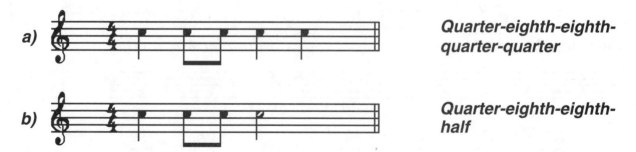

Quarter-eighth-eighth-quarter-quarter

Quarter-eighth-eighth-half

1.6. contd.

c)   *Quarter-quarter-quarter-eighth-eighth*

d)   *Half-quarter-eighth-eighth*

1.7.   In a melodic context these rhythmic patterns might occur as follows:-

KEY OF C

DO   MI SO FA   MI   SO   LA   TI   DO

KEY OF G   **KEY OF F**

DO   TI   DO   RE   MI   MI   SO   LA SO

1.8.   Notice that the total number of beats in each measure still adds up to the time signature (i.e. 4 beats). Again we can still hear the primary beats (i.e. on 1 and 3) in the above examples.

1.9.   Also in this chapter we will also discuss the D major scale, and relate it to our active/resting and resolution concepts. In the treble clef this scale is notated as follows:

(SO   LA   TI   DO)   DO   RE   MI   FA   SO   LA   TI   DO

Again note that DO has been re-assigned to the tonic of the new key i.e. the note D in this case.

1.10.   Note the key signature for D major which is two sharps (F# and C#).

1.11.   The naturally occuring resolutions (RE-DO, FA-MI, LA-SO, and TI-DO) in D major could be notated as follows:-

DO   RE   DO   DO   FA   MI   DO   LA   SO   DO   TI   DO

1.12.   Finally in this chapter we will begin our work on diatonic triad recognition. (The term 'diatonic' here means 'belonging to a key'). Diatonic triads can be built from each degree of a major scale. In the key of C these triads would be notated as follows:

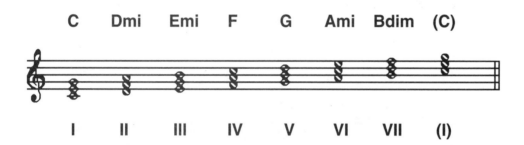

1.13.   We will begin by trying to recognize the (root position) I, IV or V triads in a key, having been given DO as a reference. See following example in the key of C:-

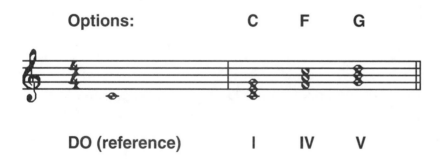

1.14. All of these major triad shapes have strong, broad and consonant interval characteristics. However each of the I, IV and V triads has different active/resting qualities depending on their respective solfeg placement, as follows:-

I triad - Always the most resting/resolved of all the diatonic triads.
(DO-MI-SO) Contains all the resting tones **DO**, **MI** and **SO**.

IV triad - Here the main active element is **FA**, which wants to resolve down
(FA-LA-DO) to **MI**. As a result the IV triad can be thought of as having a 'downward' pull or resolution energy. Also the (active whole-step) **LA** would like to resolve down to **SO**. In root position (the resting tone) **DO** is on top of the triad, which can act as a commontone or reference point.

V triad - Here the main active element is **TI**, which wants to resolve up to
(SO-TI-RE) **DO**. As a result the V triad can be thought of as having an 'upward' pull or resolution energy. Also the (active whole-step) **RE** would like to resolve to **MI** or **DO**.

2. *Class/Study Activities*

2.1. *Pitch singing and recognition*

- Singing and recognizing RE-DO, FA-MI, LA-SO and TI-DO resolutions, in the key of D.
- Individual pitch recognition in DO-DO (1 octave) range, in the key of D.

2.2. *Interval singing and recognition*

- Singing drills using minor 3rd and major 6th intervals, in the keys of C, G, and F.
- Recognition of (melodic and harmonic) minor 3rd and major 6th intervals, in the keys of C, G, and F.

2.3. *Melodic dictation/transcription*

- Transcribing melodies containing minor 3rd and major 6th intervals, using all rhythmic combinations covered so far, in the keys of C, G, and F.

2.4. *Diatonic triad recognition*

- Recognition of I, IV, or V major triads in root position, in the keys of C, G, and F.

(2.2.) <u>**VOCAL DRILLS - MINOR 3RD INTERVALS - KEY OF C**</u>

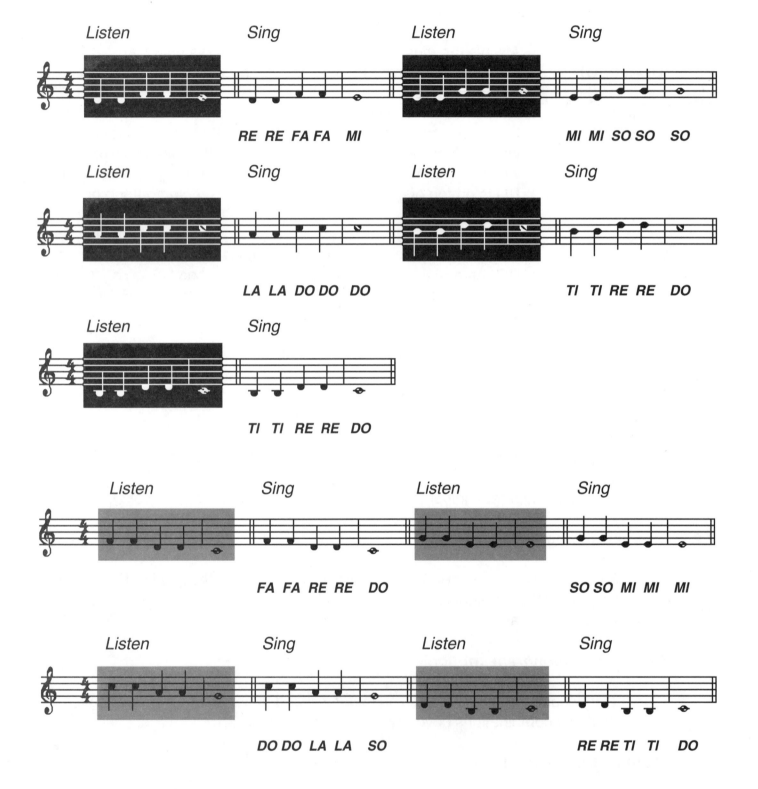

RE RE FA FA MI

MI MI SO SO SO

LA LA DO DO DO

TI TI RE RE DO

TI TI RE RE DO

FA FA RE RE DO

SO SO MI MI MI

DO DO LA LA SO

RE RE TI TI DO

(2.2. contd.)   <u>**VOCAL DRILLS - MAJOR 6TH INTERVALS - KEY OF C**</u>

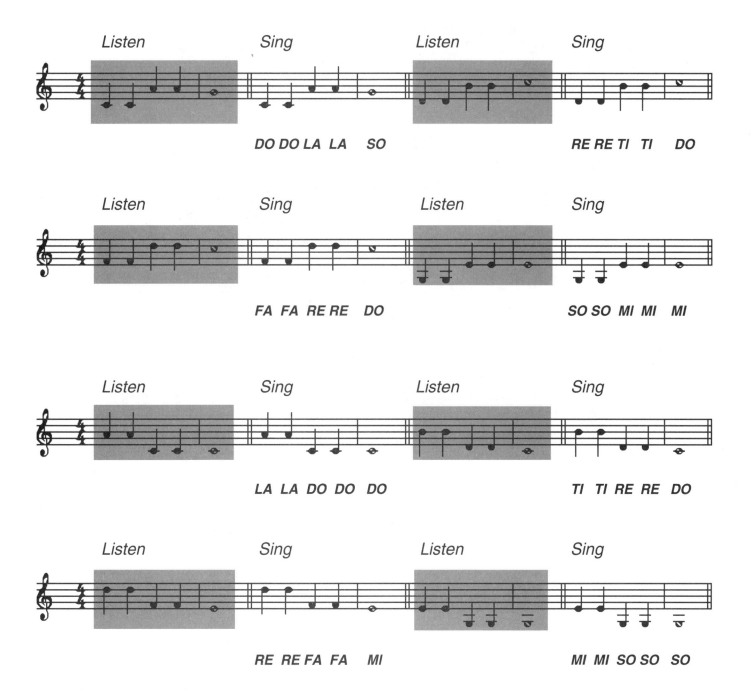

(2.2. contd.)   <u>VOCAL DRILLS - MINOR 3RD INTERVALS - KEY OF G</u>

(2.2. contd.)

VOCAL DRILLS - MAJOR 6TH INTERVALS - KEY OF G

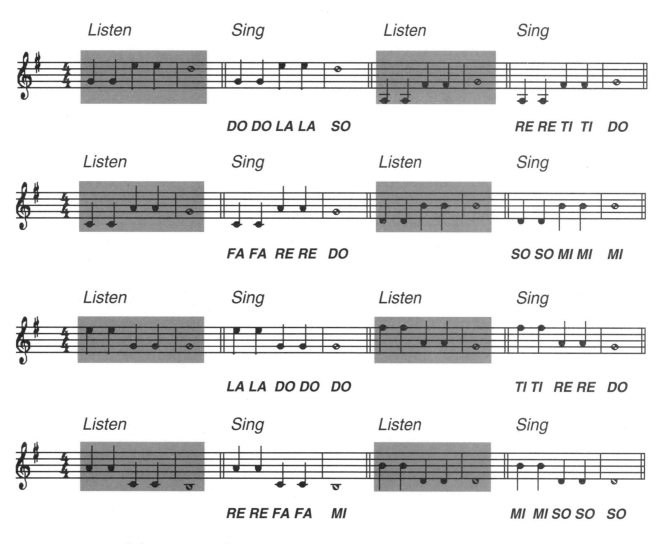

DO DO LA LA SO RE RE TI TI DO

FA FA RE RE DO SO SO MI MI MI

LA LA DO DO DO TI TI RE RE DO

RE RE FA FA MI MI MI SO SO SO

VOCAL DRILLS - MINOR 3RD INTERVALS - KEY OF F

RE RE RE FA MI MI MI MI SO SO

LA LA LA DO DO TI TI TI RE DO

(2.2. contd.) **VOCAL DRILLS - MINOR 3RD INTERVALS - KEY OF F (contd)**

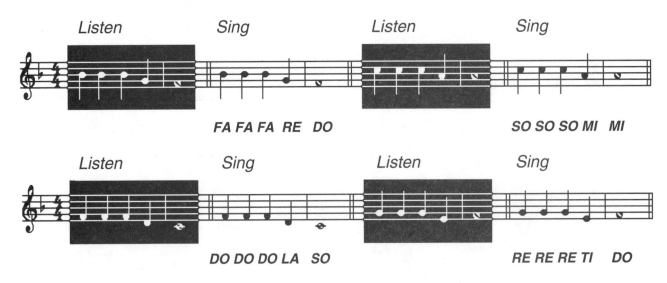

Listen *Sing* *Listen* *Sing*

FA FA FA RE DO **SO SO SO MI MI**

Listen *Sing* *Listen* *Sing*

DO DO DO LA SO **RE RE RE TI DO**

VOCAL DRILLS - MAJOR 6TH INTERVALS - KEY OF F

Listen *Sing* *Listen* *Sing*

DO DO LA LA SO **RE RE TI TI DO**

Listen *Sing* *Listen* *Sing*

FA FA RE RE DO **SO SO MI MI MI**

Listen *Sing* *Listen* *Sing*

LA LA DO DO DO **TI TI RE RE DO**

Listen *Sing* *Listen* *Sing*

RE RE FA FA MI **MI MI SO SO SO**

(2.3.)   **MELODIES FOR SINGING AND TRANSCRIPTION**

(2.3. contd)   <u>**MELODIES FOR SINGING AND TRANSCRIPTION (contd)**</u>

3. Theory Assignments

3.1. Supplementary worksheet - key of D *(p211)*.

- Write out notes on treble clef staff corresponding to the resolutions **RE-DO**, **FA-MI**, **LA-SO**, and **TI-DO**.

3.2. Supplementary worksheets - keys of C *(p193)*, **G** *(p199)*, **and F** *(p205)*.

- Write out notes on treble clef staff corresponding to the minor 3rd and major 6th intervals, ascending and descending with resolutions.

4. Eartraining Tapes Available *(see page **iv**) - tape contents for this chapter*

4.1. The Eartraining tape available for Chapter 3 consists of the following:-

- copies of the minor 3rd and major 6th interval drills in the keys of C, G, and F (see **2.2.** in text) for practice purposes

- melodic interval identification questions (minor 3rds/major 6ths) ascending and descending
    - you may fill out your answers in section **5.1.**
    - you may check against correct answers in section **6.1.**

- harmonic interval identification questions (minor 3rds/major 6ths)
    - you may fill out your answers in section **5.2.**
    - you may check against correct answers in section **6.2.**

- melodic dictation/transcription questions
    - you may fill out your answers in section **5.3.**
    - you may check against correct answers in section **6.3.**

- diatonic triad recognition
    - you may fill out your answers in section **5.4.**
    - you may check against correct answers in section **6.4.**

5. **_Eartraining Assignments - Workbook Questions_**

(fill out your answers here)

5.1. **_Melodic Interval Identification_**

Questions 1-12 consist of Minor 3rd intervals ascending or descending. The options are **RE-FA** (ascending), **FA-RE** (descending), **MI-SO** (ascending), **SO-MI** (descending), **LA-DO** (ascending), **DO-LA** (descending), **TI-RE** (ascending) or **RE-TI** (descending). Write your (solfeg) answers below:-

1. _____ _____
2. _____ _____
3. _____ _____
4. _____ _____
5. _____ _____
6. _____ _____

7. _____ _____
8. _____ _____
9. _____ _____
10. _____ _____
11. _____ _____
12. _____ _____

Questions 13-24 consist of Major 6th intervals ascending or descending. The options are **DO-LA** (ascending), **LA-DO** (descending), **RE-TI** (ascending), **TI-RE** (descending), **FA-RE** (ascending), **RE-FA** (descending), **SO-MI** (ascending) or **MI-SO** (descending). Write your (solfeg) answers below:-

13. _____ _____
14. _____ _____
15. _____ _____
16. _____ _____
17. _____ _____
18. _____ _____

19. _____ _____
20. _____ _____
21. _____ _____
22. _____ _____
23. _____ _____
24. _____ _____

(5.1. contd.)

Questions 25-44 now comprise all of the above interval possibilities (i.e. Minor 3rds and Major 6ths, ascending and descending). For each question, write the solfeg that you hear, and the interval description (either **Mi3** or **Ma6**) in parentheses:-

25. _____ _____ (   )   35. _____ _____ (   )

26. _____ _____ (   )   36. _____ _____ (   )

27. _____ _____ (   )   37. _____ _____ (   )

28. _____ _____ (   )   38. _____ _____ (   )

29. _____ _____ (   )   39. _____ _____ (   )

30. _____ _____ (   )   40. _____ _____ (   )

31. _____ _____ (   )   41. _____ _____ (   )

32. _____ _____ (   )   42. _____ _____ (   )

33. _____ _____ (   )   43. _____ _____ (   )

34. _____ _____ (   )   44. _____ _____ (   )

5.2. *Harmonic Interval Identification*

Questions 1-8 consist of Minor 3rd intervals played harmonically i.e. both tones played simultaneously. The options are **RE-FA**, **MI-SO**, **LA-DO** or **TI-RE**. Write your (solfeg) answers below:-

1. _____ _____   5. _____ _____

2. _____ _____   6. _____ _____

3. _____ _____   7. _____ _____

4. _____ _____   8. _____ _____

(5.2. contd.)

Questions 9-16 consist of Major 6th intervals played harmonically i.e. both tones played simultaneously. The options are **DO-LA**, **RE-TI**, **FA-RE** or **SO-MI**. Write your (solfeg) answers below:-

9. _____ _____   13. _____ _____

10. _____ _____   14. _____ _____

11. _____ _____   15. _____ _____

12. _____ _____   16. _____ _____

Questions 17-32 now comprise all of the above interval possibilities (i.e. harmonic Minor 3rd and Major 6th intervals). For each question, write the solfeg that you hear, and the interval description (either **Mi3** or **Ma6**) in parentheses:-

17 _____ _____ (   )   25. _____ _____ (   )

18. _____ _____ (   )   26. _____ _____ (   )

19. _____ _____ (   )   27. _____ _____ (   )

20. _____ _____ (   )   28. _____ _____ (   )

21. _____ _____ (   )   29 _____ _____ (   )

22. _____ _____ (   )   30. _____ _____ (   )

23. _____ _____ (   )   31. _____ _____ (   )

24. _____ _____ (   )   32. _____ _____ (   )

5.3.   **MELODIC DICTATION/TRANSCRIPTION**

These melodies are based upon the examples used in this chapter. *Listen for the new minor 3rd and major 6th intervals being used.* Write your answers below:-

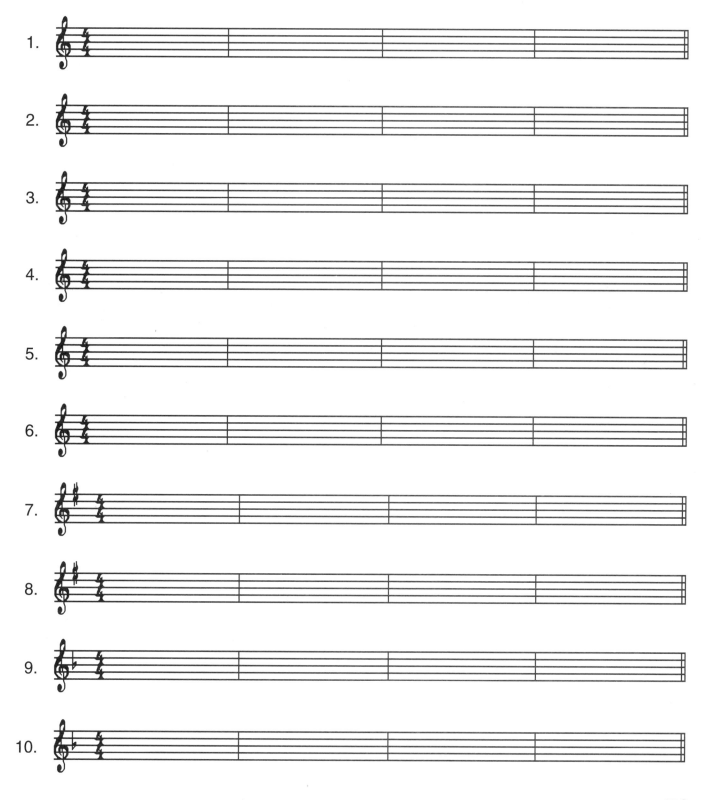

5.4. *Diatonic Triad Identification*

These questions consist of an individual root-position diatonic triad which will either be the **I**, **IV** or **V** of the respective key. Please write the chord symbol, followed by the (roman numeral) chord function in parentheses.

Questions 1-6 are in the key of C. Options are:- **C (I)**, **F (IV)**, or **G (V)**.

1. _____ (   )   4. _____ (   )

2. _____ (   )   5. _____ (   )

3. _____ (   )   6. _____ (   )

Questions 7-12 are in the key of F. Options are:- **F (I)**, **Bb (IV)**, or **C (V)**.

7. _____ (   )   10. _____ (   )

8. _____ (   )   11. _____ (   )

9. _____ (   )   12. _____ (   )

Questions 13-18 are in the key of G. Options are:- **G (I)**, **C (IV)**, or **D (V)**.

13. _____ (   )   16. _____ (   )

14. _____ (   )   17. _____ (   )

15. _____ (   )   18. _____ (   )

6. Eartraining Assignments - Workbook Answers

6.1. Melodic Interval Identification answers

(Minor 3rds)

1.	RE	-	FA	7.	DO	-	LA
2.	SO	-	MI	8.	TI	-	RE
3.	LA	-	DO	9.	FA	-	RE
4.	RE	-	TI	10.	MI	-	SO
5.	MI	-	SO	11.	LA	-	DO
6.	FA	-	RE	12.	RE	-	FA

(Major 6ths)

13.	LA	-	DO	19.	RE	-	FA
14.	RE	-	TI	20.	SO	-	MI
15.	FA	-	RE	21.	LA	-	DO
16.	MI	-	SO	22.	RE	-	FA
17.	DO	-	LA	23.	TI	-	RE
18.	TI	-	RE	24.	DO	-	LA

(Minor 3rds/Major 6ths)

25.	RE	-	TI	(Ma6)	35.	SO	-	MI	(Mi3)
26.	MI	-	SO	(Mi3)	36.	RE	-	FA	(Ma6)
27.	DO	-	LA	(Ma6)	37.	DO	-	LA	(Mi3)
28.	RE	-	FA	(Mi3)	38.	RE	-	TI	(Mi3)
29.	LA	-	DO	(Mi3)	39.	MI	-	SO	(Ma6)
30.	SO	-	MI	(Ma6)	40.	FA	-	RE	(Ma6)
31.	TI	-	RE	(Ma6)	41.	MI	-	SO	(Mi3)
32.	TI	-	RE	(Mi3)	42.	DO	-	LA	(Ma6)
33.	LA	-	DO	(Ma6)	43.	RE	-	FA	(Mi3)
34.	FA	-	RE	(Mi3)	44.	SO	-	MI	(Ma6)

6.2. Harmonic Interval Identification answers

(Minor 3rds)

1.	MI	-	SO		5.	LA	-	DO
2.	TI	-	RE		6.	TI	-	RE
3.	LA	-	DO		7.	RE	-	FA
4.	RE	-	FA		8.	MI	-	SO

(Major 6ths)

9.	RE	-	TI		13.	SO	-	MI
10.	SO	-	MI		14.	RE	-	TI
11.	DO	-	LA		15.	FA	-	RE
12.	FA	-	RE		16.	DO	-	LA

(Minor 3rds/Major 6ths)

17.	TI	-	RE	(Mi3)	25.	DO	-	LA	(Ma6)
18.	SO	-	MI	(Ma6)	26.	TI	-	RE	(Mi3)
19.	DO	-	LA	(Ma6)	27.	RE	-	TI	(Ma6)
20.	RE	-	FA	(Mi3)	28.	FA	-	RE	(Ma6)
21.	MI	-	SO	(Mi3)	29.	MI	-	SO	(Mi3)
22.	FA	-	RE	(Ma6)	30.	LA	-	DO	(Mi3)
23.	LA	-	DO	(Mi3)	31.	SO	-	MI	(Ma6)
24.	RE	-	TI	(Ma6)	32.	RE	-	FA	(Mi3)

6.3.   **MELODIC DICTATION/TRANSCRIPTION ANSWERS**

6.4. Diatonic Triad Identification answers

Key of C:

1.	*F*	(IV)		4.	*C*	(I)
2.	*C*	(I)		5.	*G*	(V)
3.	*G*	(V)		6.	*F*	(IV)

Key of F:

7.	*C*	(V)		10.	*Bb*	(IV)
8.	*Bb*	(IV)		11.	*F*	(I)
9.	*F*	(I)		12.	*C*	(V)

Key of G:

13.	*G*	(I)		16.	*G*	(I)
14.	*D*	(V)		17.	*C*	(IV)
15.	*C*	(IV)		18.	*D*	(V)

Diatonic triad melody harmonization & progressions

1.   *Theory and Notation*

1.1.   In the last chapter we introduced the D major scale, and constructed the interval resolutions which occur in the key of D major. Now we will begin to incorporate the key of D within the interval recognition drills (Major 3rds/Minor 3rds/Major 6ths/Minor 6ths) discussed so far. Refer as necessary to the Chapter 2 & 3 texts concerning the derivation of these intervals.

1.2.   In this chapter we will also further develop the subject of diatonic triads. In the last chapter we began to identify individual **I**, **IV** or **V** triads within a key. Now we will begin to identify which of the **I**, **IV** or **V** triads have been used to harmonize a melody. Consider the following melody example, in the key of C:-

The drill at this point will consist of hearing melodies such as this one, harmonized with either the **I**, **IV** or **V** triad of the key. In each case the diatonic triad is inverted to accommodate the given melody note as the top voice, with a root additionally supplied in the bass register. The previous example could have been harmonized as follows:

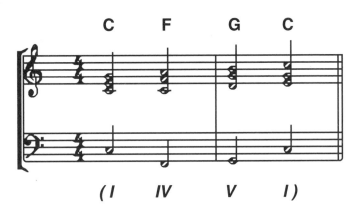

1.3.   For each melody note being harmonized, we will need to do the following:-

- establish which of the **I**, **IV** or **V** triads has been used to harmonize the melody note, and write the remaining notes of that triad below the melody note in the treble clef staff (bearing in mind that the triad may frequently be inverted)
- add a bass note (the root of the diatonic triad used) in the bass clef staff
- add a chord symbol for each diatonic triad, above the treble clef staff.

1.4.   If we are for the time being restricting ourselves to the **I**, **IV** or **V** triad for harmonization, most diatonic melody notes will only have one harmonization option. In two cases however (**DO** and **SO**) 'ear decisions' are required. Here is a summary of the options at this point:

Diatonic Melody Note		*Harmonization Options (from I, IV or V triads)*
DO	-	Choice of **I** or **IV** triad. Try to hear whether the resting tone **MI** (implying the **I** triad) or the active tone **FA** (implying the **IV** triad) is below the melody note.
RE	-	**V** triad is the only triad (within I, IV or V) containing **RE**.
MI	-	**I** triad is the only triad (within I, IV or V) containing **MI**.
FA	-	**IV** triad is the only triad (within I, IV or V) containing **FA**.
SO	-	Choice of **I** or **V** triad. Try to hear whether the resting tone **DO** (implying the **I** triad) or the active tone **TI** (implying the **V** triad) is below the melody note.
LA	-	**IV** triad is the only triad (within I, IV or V) containing **LA**.
TI	-	**V** triad is the only triad (within I, IV or V) containing **TI**.

1.5.   We will also do some work on identifying 2- and 3-chord progressions (again for now limited to the **I**, **IV** and **V** diatonic triads) for which we do not have an initial melody as a reference point. Again we will be focusing on solfeg placement and active/resting concepts (i.e. the movement between **TI-DO** and **FA-MI**) to help us derive the required chord symbols.

2.   *Class/Study Activities*

2.1.   *Interval singing and recognition*

- Singing drills using major 3rd, minor 6th, minor 3rd and major 6th intervals, in the keys of C, G and F (refer as required to Chapter 2 & Chapter 3 text)
- Recognition of above intervals (melodic and harmonic) in the keys of C, G and F.

2.2.   *Melodic dictation/transcription*

- Transcribing melodies containing major 3rd, minor 6th, minor 3rd and major 6th intervals and all rhythmic combinations covered so far, in the keys of C, G and F.

2.3.   *Diatonic triad recognition*

- Recognition of **I**, **IV**, and **V** major triads in root position, in the keys of C, G and F.
- Harmonization of 4-note melodies with **I**, **IV**, and **V** major triads, in the keys of C, G and F.
- Identifying 2- and 3-chord progressions (limited to **I**, **IV** and **V**) in the keys of C, G and F.

(2.2.)   ### MELODIES FOR SINGING AND TRANSCRIPTION

3. Theory Assignments

3.1. Supplementary worksheet - key of D *(p211).*

- Write out notes corresponding to the major 3rd, minor 6th, minor 3rd and major 6th intervals, ascending and descending with resolutions.

3.2. Supplementary worksheets - keys of C *(p193),* G *(p199),* F *(p205)* and D *(p211).*

- Write out notes on treble and bass clef staffs corresponding to the I, IV and V (major) diatonic triads.

4. Eartraining Tapes Available *(see page iv)* - tape contents for this chapter

4.1. The Eartraining tape available for Chapter 4 consists of the following:-

- melodic interval identification questions (major 3rds/minor 6ths/minor 3rds/ major 6ths) ascending and descending
    - you may fill out your answers in section **5.1.**
    - you may check against correct answers in section **6.1.**

- harmonic interval identification questions (major 3rds/minor 6ths/minor 3rds/ major 6ths)
    - you may fill out your answers in section **5.2.**
    - you may check against correct answers in section **6.2.**

- melodic dictation/transcription questions
    - you may fill out your answers in section **5.3.**
    - you may check against correct answers in section **6.3.**

- diatonic triad recognition (harmonizing 4-note melodies, and 2- & 3-chord diatonic triad progressions)
    - you may fill out your answers in section **5.4.**
    - you may check against correct answers in section **6.4.**

5. *Eartraining Assignments - Workbook Questions*

(fill out your answers here)

5.1. *Melodic Interval Identification*

Questions 1-25 consist of all possible major 3rd, minor 6th, minor 3rd and major 6th melodic intervals ascending or descending. For each question, write the solfeg that you hear, and the interval description (either **Ma3**, **Mi6**, **Mi3** or **Ma6**) in parentheses.

1. _____ _____ (   )
2. _____ _____ (   )
3. _____ _____ (   )
4. _____ _____ (   )
5. _____ _____ (   )
6. _____ _____ (   )
7. _____ _____ (   )
8. _____ _____ (   )
9. _____ _____ (   )
10. _____ _____ (   )
11. _____ _____ (   )
12. _____ _____ (   )
13. _____ _____ (   )
14. _____ _____ (   )
15. _____ _____ (   )

16. _____ _____ (   )
17. _____ _____ (   )
18. _____ _____ (   )
19. _____ _____ (   )
20. _____ _____ (   )
21. _____ _____ (   )
22. _____ _____ (   )
23. _____ _____ (   )
24. _____ _____ (   )
25. _____ _____ (   )

5.2.   *Harmonic Interval Identification*

Questions 1-16 consist of all possible Major 3rd, Minor 6th, Minor 3rd and Major 6th harmonic intervals. For each question, write the solfeg that you hear, and the interval description (either **Ma3**, **Mi6**, **Mi3** or **Ma6**) in parentheses.

1. _____ _____ (   )   9. _____ _____ (   )
2. _____ _____ (   )   10. _____ _____ (   )
3. _____ _____ (   )   11. _____ _____ (   )
4. _____ _____ (   )   12. _____ _____ (   )
5. _____ _____ (   )   13. _____ _____ (   )
6. _____ _____ (   )   14. _____ _____ (   )
7. _____ _____ (   )   15. _____ _____ (   )
8. _____ _____ (   )   16. _____ _____ (   )

5.3.   MELODIC DICTATION/TRANSCRIPTION

These questions consist of melodies based upon the material in Chapters 2 & 3. *Listen for 3rd and 6th intervals being used.* Write your answers below:-

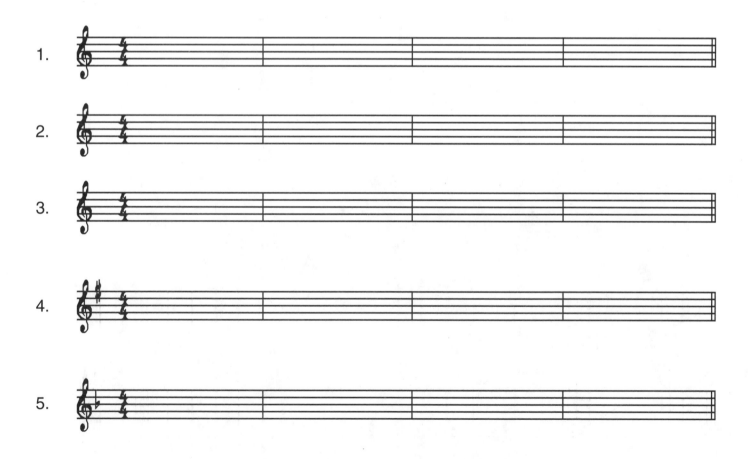

5.4. Diatonic Triad Identification

Questions 1-10 consist of melodies to which diatonic triads and bass notes are to be added. Refer to earlier text in this chapter (**1.2.-1.4.**) for instructions.

5.4. *Diatonic Triad Identification (contd)*

Questions 11-20 consist of diatonic triad 'pairs' again limited to the **I**, **IV** or **V** of the key. Write your answers (chord symbols) below:

Key of C

11. _____ _____   14. _____ _____
12. _____ _____   15. _____ _____
13. _____ _____   16. _____ _____

Key of G

17. _____ _____
18. _____ _____

Key of F

19. _____ _____
20. _____ _____

Questions 21-30 consist of progressions containing 3 triads each, again limited to the **I**, **IV** or **V** of the key. Write your answers (chord symbols) below:

Key of C

21. _____ _____ _____   24. _____ _____ _____
22. _____ _____ _____   25. _____ _____ _____
23. _____ _____ _____   26. _____ _____ _____

Key of G

27. _____ _____ _____
28. _____ _____ _____

Key of F

29. _____ _____ _____
30. _____ _____ _____

6. Eartraining Assignments - Workbook Answers

6.1. Melodic Interval Identification answers

1.	RE	-	FA	(Mi3)		14.	FA	-	RE	(Mi3)
2.	TI	-	SO	(Ma3)		15.	MI	-	SO	(Ma6)
3.	MI	-	DO	(Mi6)		16.	LA	-	FA	(MI6)
4.	FA	-	RE	(Ma6)		17.	DO	-	MI	(Mi6)
5.	FA	-	LA	(Ma3)		18.	MI	-	DO	(Ma3)
6.	LA	-	DO	(Mi3)		19.	RE	-	FA	(Ma6)
7.	RE	-	TI	(Ma6)		20.	RE	-	TI	(Mi3)
8.	TI	-	SO	(Mi6)		21.	LA	-	DO	(Ma6)
9.	MI	-	SO	(Mi3)		22.	LA	-	FA	(Ma3)
10.	DO	-	MI	(Ma3)		23.	TI	-	RE	(Mi3)
11.	LA	-	FA	(Mi6)		24.	SO	-	MI	(Mi3)
12.	DO	-	LA	(Ma6)		25.	FA	-	LA	(Ma3)
13.	SO	-	TI	(Ma3)						

6.2. Harmonic Interval Identification answers

1.	DO	-	MI	(Ma3)		9.	SO	-	TI	(Ma3)
2.	FA	-	RE	(Ma6)		10.	RE	-	TI	(Ma6)
3.	TI	-	RE	(Mi3)		11.	LA	-	DO	(Mi3)
4.	TI	-	SO	(Mi6)		12.	LA	-	FA	(Mi6)
5.	DO	-	LA	(Ma6)		13.	RE	-	FA	(Mi3)
6.	FA	-	LA	(Ma3)		14.	SO	-	MI	(Ma6)
7.	MI	-	SO	(Mi3)		15.	RE	-	TI	(Ma6)
8.	MI	-	DO	(Mi6)		16.	DO	-	MI	(Ma3)

6.3.   **MELODIC DICTATION/TRANSCRIPTION ANSWERS**

6.4.   *Diatonic Triad Identification answers*

(harmonization questions)

Key of C

6.4. Diatonic Triad Identification answers (contd)

Key of G

Key of F

(2-chord progressions)

Key of C

11.	*C*	*F*		14.	*G*	*C*
12.	*F*	*G*		15.	*F*	*C*
13.	*C*	*G*		16.	*G*	*F*

6.4. *Diatonic Triad Identification answers (contd)*

Key of G

17. *D*   *G*
18. *C*   *D*

Key of F

19. *Bb*   *F*
20. *C*   *F*

(3-chord progressions)

Key of C

21.	*F*	*G*	*C*	24.	*G*	*F*	*C*
22.	*C*	*F*	*G*	25.	*G*	*C*	*F*
23.	*C*	*G*	*F*	26.	*F*	*C*	*G*

Key of G

27. *D*   *C*   *G*
28. *C*   *D*   *G*

Key of F

29. *Bb*   *F*   *C*
30. *F*   *Bb*   *C*

4th/5th intervals, the VI diatonic triad, and bass lines

1.   Theory and Notation

1.1.   Continuing our study of the interval relationships found within a major scale, we will now focus on the diatonic perfect 4th, augmented 4th, perfect 5th and diminished 5th intervals. The perfect 4th has a span of two-and-a-half steps (or 5 half-steps). The perfect 5th has a span of three-and-a-half steps (or 7 half-steps) and is the inversion of the perfect 4th. The augmented 4th and diminished 5th both have a span of three whole steps (or 6 half-steps) and can be derived by dividing an octave in half. These intervals can also be referred to as a 'tritones' due to their span of three whole-steps.

1.2.   These are the melodic perfect 4th, augmented 4th, perfect 5th and diminished 5th intervals present in the major scale (shown in the 3 most recent keys studied - **G**, **F** and **D**):-

KEY OF G

Melodic Perfect 4ths Ascending

DO FA (MI)   RE SO MI LA (SO)   SO DO LA RE (DO)   TI MI

Melodic Perfect 4ths Descending

FA DO SO RE (DO)   LA MI DO SO RE LA (SO)   MI TI (DO)

Melodic Perfect 5ths Ascending

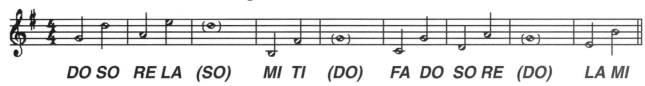

DO SO RE LA (SO)   MI TI (DO)   FA DO SO RE (DO)   LA MI

Melodic Perfect 5ths Descending

SO DO LA RE (DO)   TI MI DO FA (MI)   RE SO MI LA (SO)

1.2. contd.   <u>KEY OF G (contd)</u>

Melodic Aug 4ths/Dim 5ths Ascending   *Melodic Aug 4ths/Dim 5ths Descending*

FA TI (DO)   TI FA (MI)   TI FA (MI)   FA TI (DO)

<u>KEY OF F</u>

Melodic Perfect 4ths Ascending

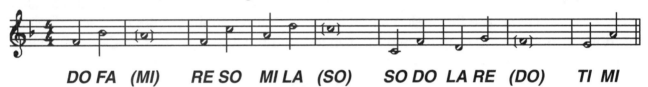

DO FA (MI)   RE SO   MI LA (SO)   SO DO LA RE (DO)   TI MI

Melodic Perfect 4ths Descending

FA DO SO RE (DO)   LA MI DO SO RE LA (SO)   MI TI (DO)

Melodic Perfect 5ths Ascending

DO SO RE LA (SO)   MI TI (DO)   FA DO SO RE (DO)   LA MI

Melodic Perfect 5ths Descending

SO DO LA RE (DO)   TI MI DO FA (MI)   RE SO MI LA (SO)

Melodic Aug 4ths/Dim 5ths Ascending   *Melodic Aug 4ths/Dim 5ths Descending*

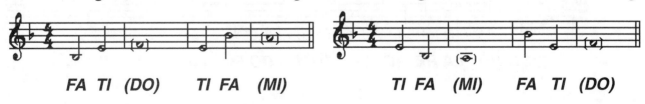

FA TI (DO)   TI FA (MI)   TI FA (MI)   FA TI (DO)

1.2. contd. <u>**KEY OF D**</u>

Melodic Perfect 4ths Ascending

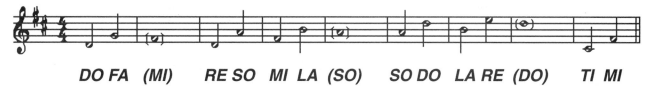

DO FA (MI) RE SO MI LA (SO) SO DO LA RE (DO) TI MI

Melodic Perfect 4ths Descending

FA DO SO RE (DO) LA MI DO SO RE LA (SO) MI TI (DO)

Melodic Perfect 5ths Ascending

DO SO RE LA (SO) MI TI (DO) FA DO SO RE (DO) LA MI

Melodic Perfect 5ths Descending

SO DO LA RE (DO) TI MI DO FA (MI) RE SO MI LA (SO)

Melodic Aug 4ths/Dim 5ths Ascending   *Melodic Aug 4ths/Dim 5ths Descending*

FA TI (DO) TI FA (MI)   TI FA (MI) FA TI (DO)

As with the intervals introduced in previous chapters, note that when an interval ends on an active tone, the natural resolution from that active tone to the appropriate resting tone is also shown i.e. **DO - FA**, resolving to **MI**.

1.3.   These are the harmonic perfect 4th, perfect 5th and augmented 4th/diminished 5th intervals present within the major scale (again shown in the keys of G, F and D):

KEY OF G

Harmonic Perfect 4ths

FA	SO	LA	DO	RE	MI
DO	RE	MI	SO	LA	TI

Harmonic Augmented 4ths/ Diminished 5ths

TI	FA
FA	TI

Harmonic Perfect 5ths

SO	LA	TI	DO	RE	MI
DO	RE	MI	FA	SO	LA

KEY OF F

Harmonic Perfect 4ths

FA	SO	LA	DO	RE	MI
DO	RE	MI	SO	LA	TI

Harmonic Augmented 4ths/ Diminished 5ths

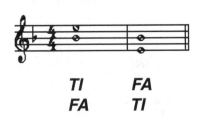

TI	FA
FA	TI

Harmonic Perfect 5ths

SO	LA	TI	DO	RE	MI
DO	RE	MI	FA	SO	LA

1.3. contd.

KEY OF D

Harmonic Perfect 4ths

FA	SO	LA	DO	RE	MI
DO	RE	MI	SO	LA	TI

Harmonic Augmented 4ths/
Diminished 5ths

TI	FA
FA	TI

Harmonic Perfect 5ths

SO	LA	TI	DO	RE	MI
DO	RE	MI	FA	SO	LA

1.4.　　　　The perfect 4th and perfect 5th intervals illustrated above have rather different characteristics from the previously discussed diatonic 3rd and 6th intervals. Melodically these 4th and 5th intervals have a strong, leading and 'tonal' impression. The top note of a 4th interval, and the bottom note of a 5th interval, can sound like a new '**DO**' or tonal center, due to the implied dominant/tonic relationship inherent in perfect 4th/5th intervals. While this is a useful trick to distinguish these intervals, it is of course important to keep track of where **DO** really is during this process! Harmonically both of these intervals have a consonant and 'hollow' impression, with the 5th of course having a larger span. You might find it helpful to think of the (harmonic) 5th interval as a root position triad with the 3rd missing - the (harmonic) 4th on the other hand could represent adjacent tones in an inverted triad. Also the harmonic perfect 4th interval could subjectively be thought of as having a more 'oriental' impression.

1.5.　　　　By contrast the augmented 4th/diminished 5th/tritone interval has rather opposite characteristics. This interval *always sounds active* as it always contains the two most active scale tones (**TI** and **FA**) of the major scale. Melodically this interval sounds very angular and non-leading. Harmonically this interval sounds dissonant and typically requires resolution.

1.6.　　　　All perfect 4th and perfect 5th intervals will consist of either **DO-FA**, **RE-SO**, **MI-LA**, **SO-DO**, **LA-RE** or **TI-MI** pairs of notes. In addition to the above mentioned interval characteristics, there will also be differences in impression due to the respective active/resting qualities:-

75

1.6. contd.

DO-FA/
FA-DO

DO is a resting tone and **FA** is an active tone. Melodically when ending on **FA** (ascending perfect 4th/descending perfect 5th) the interval will want to resolve to **MI**. When ending on **DO** (ascending perfect 5th/descending perfect 4th) the interval will not need resolution as we have landed on the resting tone **DO**. However this is something of an 'unprepared' resolution as we have not resolved into **DO** via an adjacent active tone (despite the 'leading' interval quality).

RE-SO/
SO-RE

RE is an active tone and **SO** is a resting tone. Melodically when ending on **RE** (ascending perfect 5th/descending perfect 4th) the interval will want to resolve to **DO** (or **MI**). When ending on **SO** (ascending perfect 4th/descending perfect 5th) the interval will not need resolution as we have landed on the resting tone **SO**. However this is something of an 'unprepared' resolution as we have not resolved into **SO** via an adjacent active tone (despite the 'leading' interval quality).

MI-LA/
LA-MI

MI is a resting tone and **LA** is an active tone. Melodically when ending on **LA** (ascending perfect 4th/descending perfect 5th) the interval will want to resolve to **SO**. When ending on **MI** (ascending perfect 5th/descending perfect 4th) the interval will not need resolution as we have landed on the resting tone **MI**. However this is something of an 'unprepared' resolution as we have not resolved into **MI** via an adjacent active tone (despite the 'leading' interval quality).

SO-DO/
DO-SO

Always the most resting or stable perfect 4th/perfect 5th interval. Both of these tones are resting tones.

LA-RE/
RE-LA

Both of these tones are active, creating an active interval. Melodically when ending on **RE** (ascending perfect 4th/descending perfect 5th) the interval will want to resolve to **DO** (or **MI**). When ending on **LA** (ascending perfect 5th/descending perfect 4th) the interval will want to resolve to **SO**.

TI-MI/
MI-TI

MI is a resting tone and **TI** is an active tone. Melodically when ending on **TI** (ascending perfect 5th/descending perfect 4th) the interval will want to resolve to **DO**. When ending on **MI** (ascending perfect 4th/descending perfect 5th) the interval will not need resolution as we have landed on the resting tone **MI**. However this is something of an 'unprepared' resolution as we have not resolved into **MI** via an adjacent active tone (despite the 'leading' interval quality).

1.7. Also in this chapter we will introduce some more rhythmic combinations featuring pairs of eighth notes. (Remember that each eighth note lasts for half a beat, and when they are written in pairs they will be 'beamed' together). Consider the following new rhythms:-

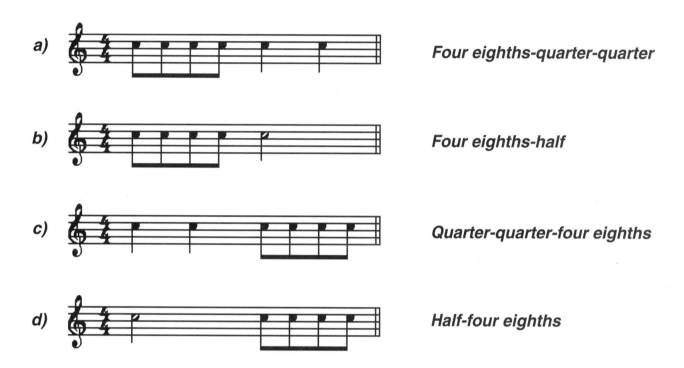

a) Four eighths-quarter-quarter

b) Four eighths-half

c) Quarter-quarter-four eighths

d) Half-four eighths

1.8. In a melodic context these rhythmic patterns might occur as follows:-

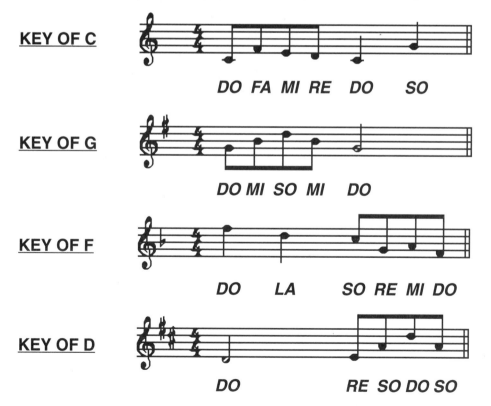

KEY OF C

DO FA MI RE DO SO

KEY OF G

DO MI SO MI DO

KEY OF F

DO LA SO RE MI DO

KEY OF D

DO RE SO DO SO

1.9. Also in this chapter we will continue our work on diatonic triad recognition, by adding the **VI minor** triad to the available possibilities as follows (key of C):

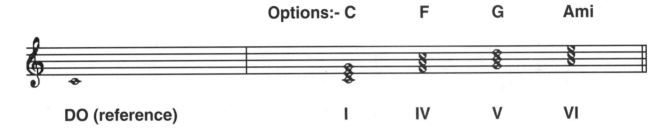

(Refer to Chapter 3 text, paragraph **1.14.** for characteristics of the **I**, **IV** and **V** triads)

1.10. The **VI minor** diatonic triad (containing **LA-DO-MI**) can be recognized as follows:-

CHORD QUALITY - The minor triad, while having a consonant impression (like major) has a darker or more mellow sound than major due to the minor 3rd interval between the root and 3rd of the triad. Sometimes (rather subjectively!) the terms 'happy' and 'sad' are used to contrast the impressions of the major and minor triads respectively.

ACTIVE/RESTING QUALITIES - The VI minor is the most resting of all the diatonic triads apart from the I major. Neither of the most active tones (**TI** or **FA**) are present. **DO** and **MI** are fully resting, and **LA** is only a semi-active tone (or 'active whole-step').

1.11. We will also extend our 'melody harmonization' and 'chord progression' diatonic triad exercises to now include the **VI minor** triad. For the melody harmonization (refer to Chapter 4 text paragraph **1.4.**), this now adds to the 'ear decisions' required, as follows:

DIATONIC MELODY NOTE	*DIATONIC TRIAD HARMONIZATION OPTIONS*
DO	*I Major* (i.e. **C** in the key of C) *IV Major* (i.e. **F** in the key of C) *VI Minor* (i.e. **Ami** in the key of C)
RE	*V Major* (i.e. **G** in the key of C)
MI	*I Major* (i.e. **C** in the key of C) *VI Minor* (i.e. **Ami** in the key of C)
FA	*IV Major* (i.e. **F** in the key of C)

1.11. contd.

DIATONIC MELODY NOTE	DIATONIC TRIAD HARMONIZATION OPTIONS
SO	*I Major* (i.e. **C** in the key of C) *V Major* (i.e. **G** in the key of C)
LA	*IV Major* (i.e. **F** in the key of C) *VI Minor* (i.e. **Ami** in the key of C)
TI	*V Major* (i.e. **G** in the key of C)

As before, we will be combining our sense of diatonic triad 'chord quality' with hearing the active/resting nature of each triad, in order to do these harmonization and progression exercises.

1.12.   In this chapter we will also discuss the **Bb** major scale, and relate it to our active/resting concepts. In the treble clef this scale is notated as follows:-

(SO   LA   TI   DO)   DO   RE   MI   FA   SO   LA   TI   DO

1.13.   Note the key signature for Bb major which is two flats (Bb and Eb).

1.14.   The naturally-occurring resolutions (**RE-DO**, **FA-MI**, **LA-SO** and **TI-DO**) in Bb major could be notated as follows:

DO   RE   DO   DO   FA   MI   DO   LA   SO   DO   TI   DO

DO   LA   SO   DO   TI   DO

1.15.   Finally in this chapter we will begin our work on bass line dictation. As part of the 'melody harmonization' exercises with diatonic triads, you will already have been detecting and transcribing voices in the bass register. Now, we will begin to focus on some of the 'linear' aspects of bass lines. Our starting point will be to consider bass lines as melodies in the bass register. As such they will exhibit all the normal active/resting qualities and interval relationships that we would normally associate with a melody. However, additional information is available via studying root interval qualities, harmonic implications and any melodic/harmonic repetition or 'pattern' elements.

1.16.   We have already seen from our studies of perfect 4th/perfect 5th intervals (see paragraph **1.4.** earlier in this chapter) that these intervals melodically have a leading and 'tonal' impression. When used in the bass register these intervals sound especially strong and stable. Consider the following example:

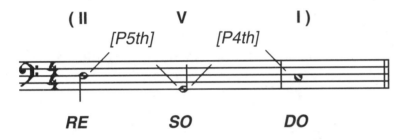

Here the very strong and leading impression is casued by the successive 5th/4th intervals, creating a 'circle-of-fifths' type of motion (more of this in **Contemporary Eartraining Level 2**).

1.17.   The root interval of a half-step, while much smaller in span than the perfect 4th/perfect 5th, is also considered to be strong, leading and 'tonal' in nature. Other root intervals are considered 'symmetric' as they are the result of dividing an octave into an equal number of parts, or inversions thereof. (For example:- a Major 3rd can be derived by dividing an octave into 3 equal parts. The Minor 6th is the inversion of the Major 3rd. Both of these root intervals would be considered 'symmetric'). Symmetric root intervals are rather less leading and predictable in nature, and create a different stylistic effect when used in bass lines.

1.18.   Among the 'symmetric' root interval choices, the Major 3rd and Minor 3rd intervals are frequently encountered in contemporary styles. Consider the following example:

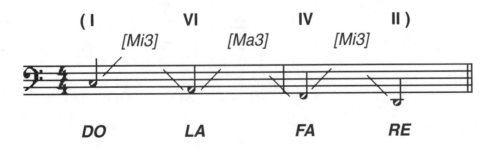

(1.18. contd.)

Here the successive diatonic 3rd intervals have a melodic effect, but the overall impression is rather less strong and leading than the previous **RE-SO-DO** bassline for example.

1.19. One other root interval relationship we will consider, could be termed 'scalewise' movement. Whenever the line consists of two or more adjacent scale steps ascending or descending, this has a melodic effect which reinforces the scale or key center. (Technically, this movement combines 'symmetric' whole-steps with 'tonal' half-steps). Consider the following example:

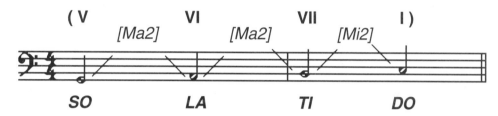

The 'scalewise' root movement (in this case ending with a **TI-DO** resolution) is the predominant impression from bass lines of this nature.

1.20. There are some additional aspects to bass lines that we need to consider. As we do bass line dictation, we should also evaluate the 'harmonic implications' of the bass line. At this level the chord implied will be one of the diatonic triads available within the key center. We know that the strong beats of a **4/4** measure occur on **1** and **3**. It is on these points that we would expect to hear a basic chord tone (either root, 3rd or 5th) of a diatonic triad, in simpler contemporary styles. Diatonic passing tones may be supplied on the weak beats of the measure. Also the bass line may involve elements of rhythmic and melodic repetition (very common in contemporary applications). With these points in mind, let us consider the following example:

In the first measure, we hear **DO** and **SO** on the strong beats (**1** and **3**). We know this is the root and fifth of the **I** triad (C major) and so the harmonic implication is likely to be **C** for a measure. Now we focus on the weak beats and hear the scalewise movement either side of **SO** on beat **3** - this is **LA** functioning as a diatonic 'passing tone' (and is the 6th of the implied **C** major chord). Then we hear the repeated root-sixth-fifth-sixth pattern starting on **SO** in the second measure - here the harmonic implication is likely to be **G** for a measure. Finally the line ends on the resting tone **DO** in the third measure, again implying a **C** major chord during this measure.

1.21.   In drilling on bass lines we will therefore be focusing on the following areas:-

-    active/resting qualities

-    root interval qualities

  -    'tonal'
  -    'symmetric'
  -    'scalewise'

-    harmonic implication

-    melodic/harmonic pattern or repetition elements

2.   *Class/Study Activities*

2.1.   *Interval singing and recognition*

-    Singing drills using perfect 4th, perfect 5ths, augmented 4th and diminished 5th intervals, in the keys of F and D.
-    Recognition of (melodic and harmonic) all interval types covered so far, in the keys of C, G, F and D.

2.2.   *Melodic dictation/transcription*

-    Transcribing melodies containing perfect 4th, perfect 5th, augmented 4th and diminished 5th intervals, using all rhythmic combinations covered so far, in the keys of C, G and F.
-    Transcribing melodies using simpler rhythms and intervals, in the key of D.

2.3.   *Diatonic triad recognition*

-    Recognition of **I**, **IV**, **V** and **VI** diatonic triads in root position, in the keys of C, G, and F.
-    Harmonization of (given) 4-note melodies with **I**, **IV**, **V** or **VI** diatonic triads, in the keys of C, G, F and D.
-    Identifying 2- and 3-chord progressions limited to the **I**, **IV**, **V** and **VI** diatonic triads, in the keys of C, G and F.

2.4.   *Bass line dictation/transcription*

-    Transcribing bass lines containing whole note, half-note and quarter note rhythms, in the keys of C, G and F.

(2.1.) **VOCAL DRILLS - PERFECT 4th and AUGMENTED 4th INTERVALS - KEY OF F**

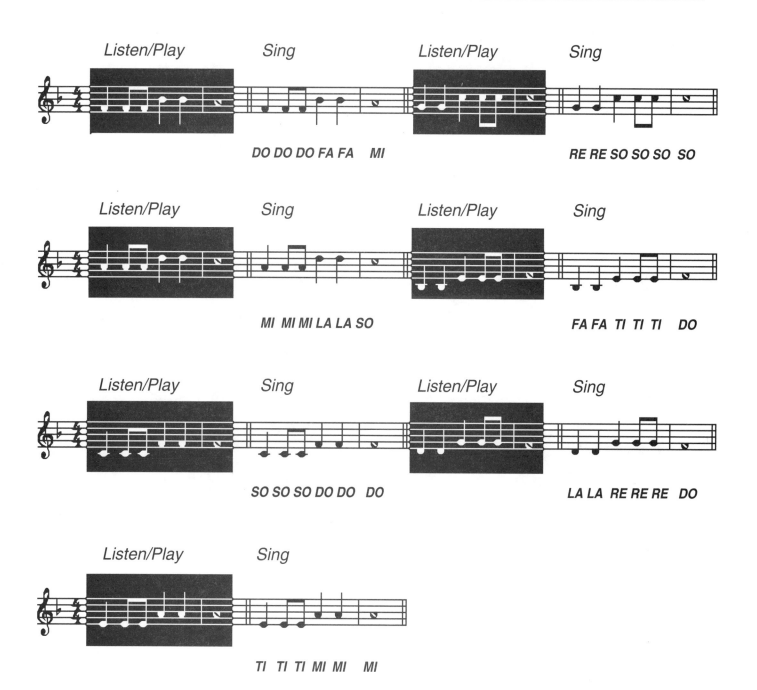

DO DO DO FA FA   MI

RE RE SO SO SO SO

MI MI MI LA LA SO

FA FA TI TI TI   DO

SO SO SO DO DO DO

LA LA RE RE RE DO

TI TI TI MI MI   MI

(2.1. contd)   <u>VOCAL DRILLS - PERFECT 4th and AUGMENTED 4th INTERVALS</u>
<u>- KEY OF F (contd)</u>

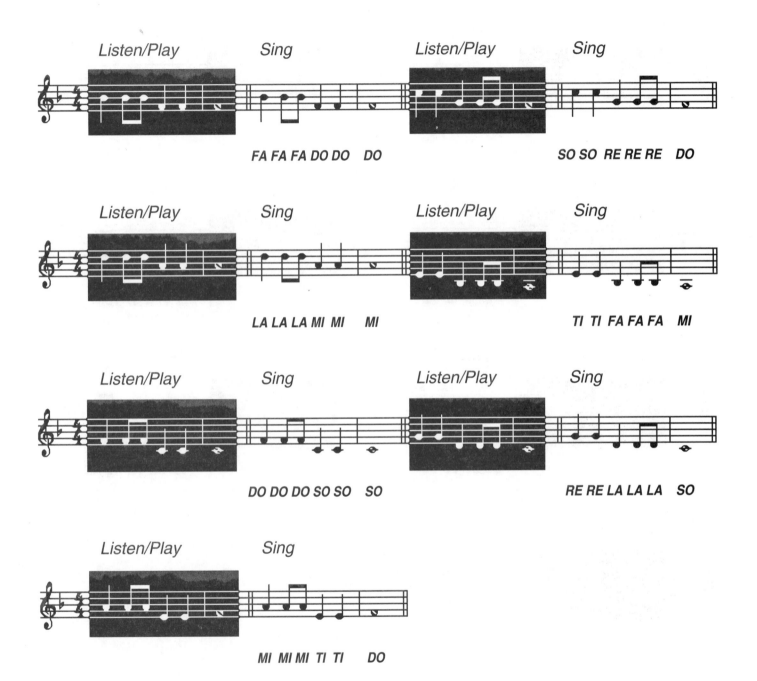

(2.1. contd) <u>VOCAL DRILLS - PERFECT 5th and DIMINISHED 5th INTERVALS - KEY OF F</u>

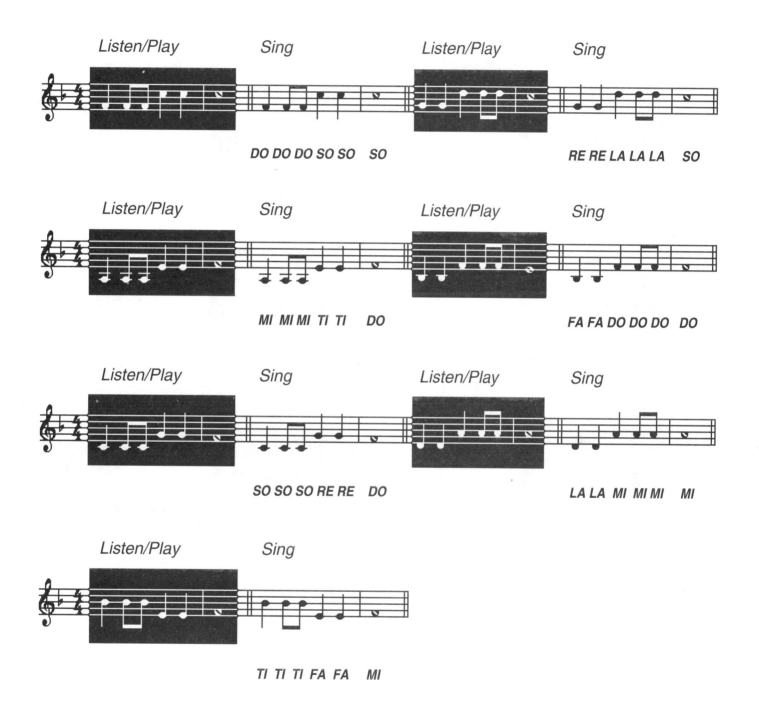

DO DO DO SO SO   SO

RE RE LA LA LA   SO

MI MI MI TI TI   DO

FA FA DO DO DO   DO

SO SO SO RE RE   DO

LA LA MI MI MI   MI

TI TI TI FA FA   MI

(2.1. contd) **VOCAL DRILLS - PERFECT 5th and DIMINISHED 5th INTERVALS - KEY OF F (contd)**

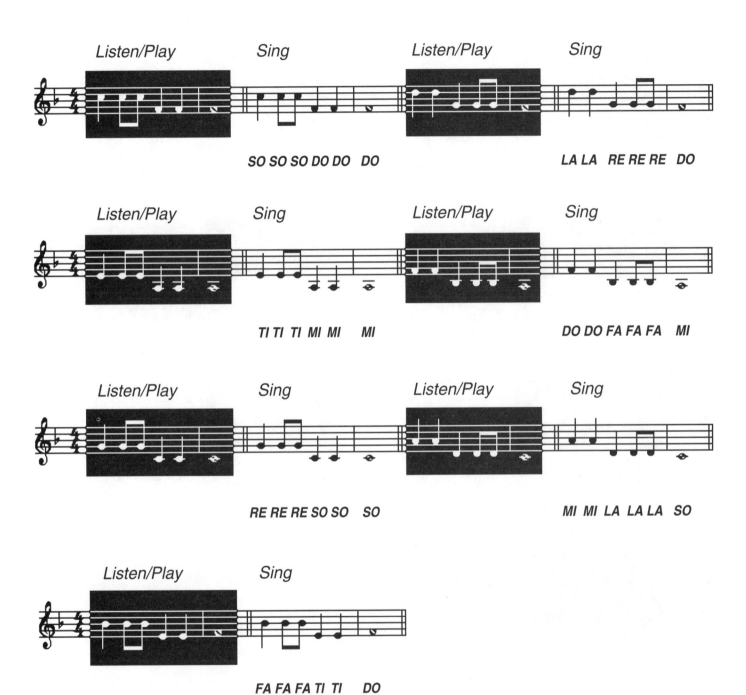

SO SO SO DO DO DO

LA LA RE RE RE DO

TI TI TI MI MI   MI

DO DO FA FA FA   MI

RE RE RE SO SO   SO

MI MI LA LA LA SO

FA FA FA TI TI   DO

(2.1. contd) <u>VOCAL DRILLS - PERFECT 4th and AUGMENTED 4th INTERVALS - KEY OF D</u>

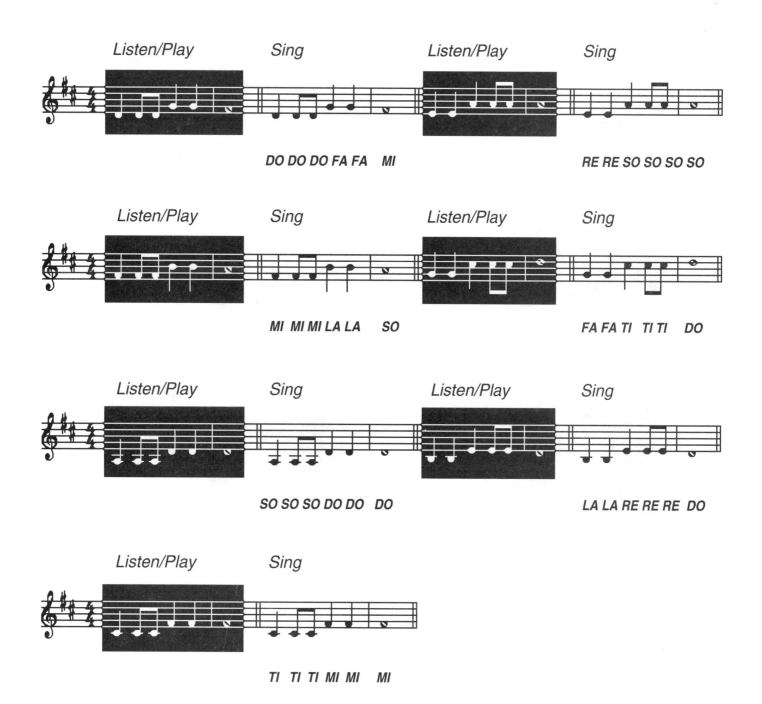

DO DO DO FA FA   MI   RE RE SO SO SO SO

MI MI MI LA LA   SO   FA FA TI TI TI   DO

SO SO SO DO DO   DO   LA LA RE RE RE DO

TI TI TI MI MI   MI

(2.1. contd) **VOCAL DRILLS - PERFECT 4th and AUGMENTED 4th INTERVALS - KEY OF D (contd)**

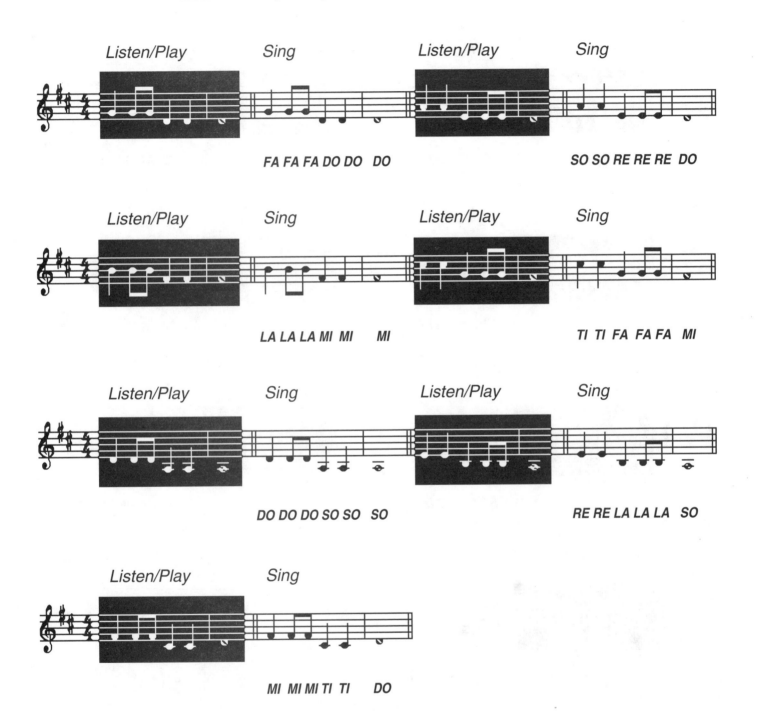

FA FA FA DO DO DO

SO SO RE RE RE DO

LA LA LA MI MI   MI

TI TI FA FA FA   MI

DO DO DO SO SO   SO

RE RE LA LA LA   SO

MI MI MI TI TI   DO

(2.1. contd) <u>VOCAL DRILLS - PERFECT 5th and DIMINISHED 5th INTERVALS - KEY OF D</u>

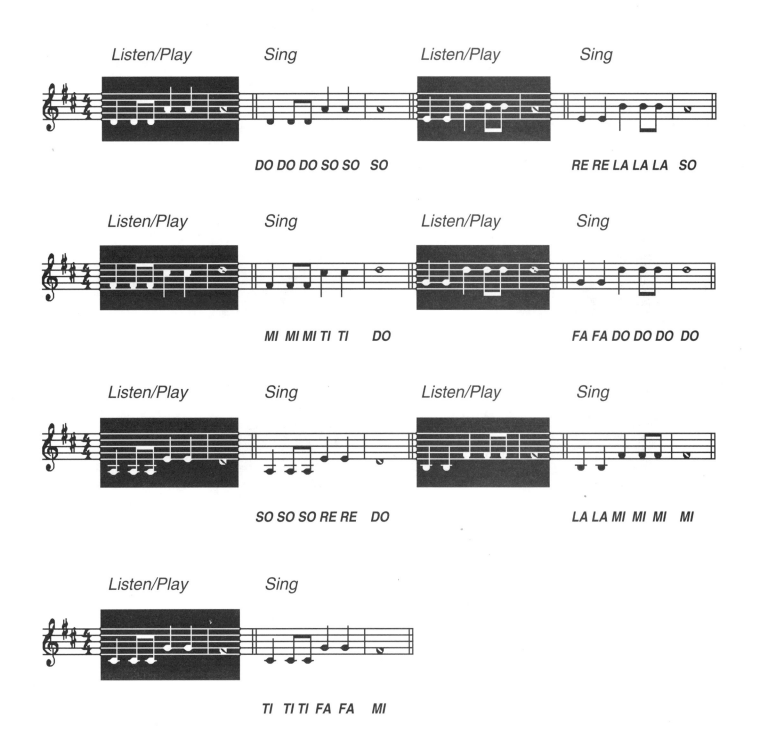

(2.1. contd)   **VOCAL DRILLS - PERFECT 5th and DIMINISHED 5th INTERVALS - KEY OF D (contd)**

SO SO SO DO DO DO

LA LA RE RE RE DO

TI TI TI MI MI MI

DO DO FA FA FA MI

RE RE RE SO SO SO

MI MI LA LA LA SO

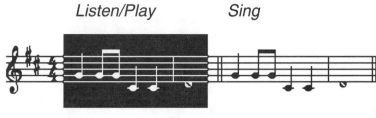

FA FA FA TI TI DO

(2.2.)   **<u>MELODIES FOR SINGING AND TRANSCRIPTION</u>**

(2.2. contd) **MELODIES FOR SINGING AND TRANSCRIPTION (contd)**

3. Theory Assignments

3.1. Supplementary worksheets - keys of C (p193), G (p199), F (p205) and D (p211).

- Write out notes on treble clef staff corresponding to the perfect 4th, perfect 5th, augmented 4th and diminished 5th melodic (ascending and descending) and harmonic intervals.
- Write out notes on treble and bass clef staffs corresponding to the **VI minor** diatonic triad.

3.2. Supplementary worksheet - key of Bb (p217).

- Write out notes on treble clef staff corresponding to the following:-
    - lower and upper tetrachords with resolutions
    - all 3rd, 4th, 5th and 6th melodic (ascending and descending) and harmonic intervals
- Write out notes on treble and bass clef staffs corresponding to the **I**, **IV**, **V** and **VI minor** diatonic triads.

4. Eartraining Tapes Available (see page iv) - tape contents for this chapter

4.1. The Eartraining tape available for Chapter 5 consists of the following:-

- melodic interval identification questions (perfect 4ths/perfect 5ths/augmented 4ths/diminished 5ths) ascending and descending
    - you may fill out your answers in section **5.1.**
    - you may check against correct answers in section **6.1.**

- harmonic interval identification questions (perfect 4ths/perfect 5ths/augmented 4ths/diminished 5ths)
    - you may fill out your answers in section **5.2.**
    - you may check against correct answers in section **6.2.**

- melodic dictation/transcription questions
    - you may fill out your answers in section **5.3.**
    - you may check against correct answers in section **6.3.**

- diatonic triad recognition (individual triads, harmonizing 4-note melodies, and 2- and 3-chord progressions)
    - you may fill out your answers in section **5.4.**
    - you may check against correct answers in section **6.4.**

(4.1. contd)

- bass line dictation/transcription
  - fill out your answers in section **5.5.**
  - check against correct answers in section **6.5.**

5. **_Eartraining Assignments - Workbook Questions_**

(fill out your answers here)

5.1. **_Melodic Interval Identification_**

Questions 1-12 consist of perfect 4th or augmented 4th intervals ascending or descending. The options are:-

DO-FA (perfect 4th ascending),   **RE-SO** (perfect 4th ascending),
MI-LA (perfect 4th ascending),   **FA-TI** (augmented 4th ascending),
SO-DO (perfect 4th ascending),   **LA-RE** (perfect 4th ascending),
TI-MI (perfect 4th ascending),   **FA-DO** (perfect 4th descending),
SO-RE (perfect 4th descending),   **LA-MI** (perfect 4th descending),
TI-FA (augmented 4th descending), **DO-SO** (perfect 4th descending),
RE-LA (perfect 4th descending), or **MI-TI** (perfect 4th descending).

Write your (solfeg) answers below and indicate (Per4) or (Aug4) in parentheses:-

1. _____ _____ ( )	7. _____ _____ ( )
2. _____ _____ ( )	8. _____ _____ ( )
3. _____ _____ ( )	9. _____ _____ ( )
4. _____ _____ ( )	10. _____ _____ ( )
5. _____ _____ ( )	11. _____ _____ ( )
6. _____ _____ ( )	12. _____ _____ ( )

Questions 13-24 consist of perfect 5th or diminished 5th intervals ascending or descending. The options are:-

DO-SO (perfect 5th ascending),   **RE-LA** (perfect 5th ascending),
MI-TI (perfect 5th ascending),   **FA-DO** (perfect 5th ascending),
SO-RE (perfect 5th ascending),   **LA-MI** (perfect 5th ascending),
TI-FA (diminished 5th ascending),   **SO-DO** (perfect 5th descending),
LA-RE (perfect 5th descending),   **TI-MI** (perfect 5th descending),
DO-FA (perfect 5th descending),   **RE-SO** (perfect 5th descending),
MI-LA (perfect 5th descending), or **FA-TI** (diminished 5th descending).

(5.1. contd)

Write your (solfeg) answers below and indicate (Per5) or (Dim5) in parentheses:-

13. ____ ____ ( )		19. ____ ____ ( )	
14. ____ ____ ( )		20. ____ ____ ( )	
15. ____ ____ ( )		21. ____ ____ ( )	
16. ____ ____ ( )		22. ____ ____ ( )	
17. ____ ____ ( )		23. ____ ____ ( )	
18. ____ ____ ( )		24. ____ ____ ( )	

Questions 25-40 now comprise all of the above interval possibilities (i.e. perfect 4ths, perfect 5ths, augmented 4ths and diminished 5ths ascending and descending). For each question, write the notes on the staff, together with the solfeg and interval description.

25. 26. 27. 28.

Key of C

Solfeg:
Interval Description:

29. 30. 31. 32.

Key of G

Solfeg:
Interval Description:

33. 34. 35. 36.

Key of F

Solfeg:
Interval Description:

(5.1. contd)

37.   38.   39.   40.

Key of D

Solfeg: ____ ____   ____ ____   ____ ____   ____ ____
Interval Description: _____   _____   _____   _____

(Questions 41-50 now include all intervals studied prior to this chapter, within the range of possibilities).

41.   42.   43.   44.   45.

Key of C

Solfeg: ____ ____   ____ ____   ____ ____   ____ ____   ____ ____
Interval Description: _____   _____   _____   _____   _____

46.   47.   48.   49.   50.

Key of G

Solfeg: ____ ____   ____ ____   ____ ____   ____ ____   ____ ____
Interval Description: _____   _____   _____   _____   _____

5.2. Harmonic Interval Identification

Questions 1-8 consist of perfect 4th and augmented 4th intervals played harmonically i.e. both tones played simultaneously. The options are **DO-FA** (perfect 4th), **RE-SO** (perfect 4th), **MI-LA** (perfect 4th), **FA-TI** (augmented 4th), **SO-DO** (perfect 4th), **LA-RE** (perfect 4th), and **TI-MI** (perfect 4th). Write your (solfeg) answers below and indicate (per4) or (aug4) in parentheses:-

1. ____ ____ (   )   5. ____ ____ (   )
2. ____ ____ (   )   6. ____ ____ (   )
3. ____ ____ (   )   7. ____ ____ (   )
4. ____ ____ (   )   8. ____ ____ (   )

(5.2. contd)

Questions 9-16 consist of perfect 5th and diminished 5th intervals played harmonically. The options are **DO-SO** (perfect 5th), **RE-LA** (perfect 5th), **MI-TI** (perfect 5th), **FA-DO** (perfect 5th), **SO-RE** (perfect 5th), **LA-MI** (perfect 5th), and **TI-FA** (diminished 5th). Write your (solfeg) answers below and indicate (per5) or (dim5) in parentheses:-

9. _____ _____ (   )   13. _____ _____ (   )
10. _____ _____ (   )   14. _____ _____ (   )
11. _____ _____ (   )   15. _____ _____ (   )
12. _____ _____ (   )   16. _____ _____ (   )

Questions 17-28 now comprise all of the above interval possibilities (i.e. harmonic perfect 4ths, perfect 5ths, augmented 4ths and diminished 5ths). For each question, write the notes on the staff, together with the solfeg and interval description:-

17.   18.   19.   20.

Key of C

Solfeg: _____ _____   _____ _____   _____ _____   _____ _____
Interval Description: _____   _____   _____   _____

21.   22.   23.   24.

Key of G

Solfeg: _____ _____   _____ _____   _____ _____   _____ _____
Interval Description: _____   _____   _____   _____

25.   26.   27.   28.

Key of F

Solfeg: _____ _____   _____ _____   _____ _____   _____ _____
Interval Description: _____   _____   _____   _____

(5.2. contd)

(Questions 29-36 now include all intervals studied prior to this chapter, within the range of possibilities).

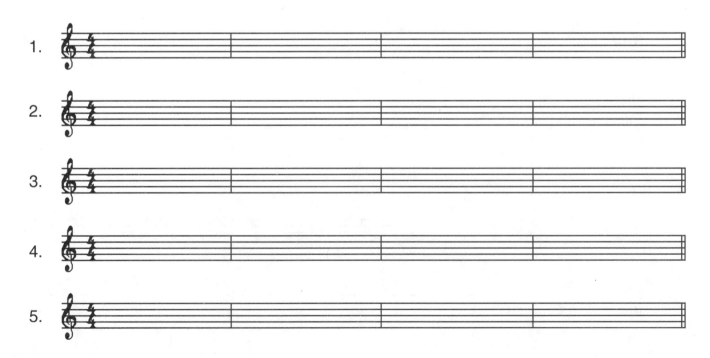

29.   30.   31.   32.

Key of C

Solfeg:
Interval Description:

33.   34.   35.   36.

Key of G

Solfeg:
Interval Description:

5.3.   **MELODIC DICTATION/TRANSCRIPTION**

These 10 questions consist of melodies based on this chapter's material. *Listen for the new 4th and 5th intervals being used.* Write your answers below:-

1.

2.

3.

4.

5.

(5.3. contd) **MELODIC DICTATION/TRANSCRIPTION contd.**

6.

7.

8.

9.

10.

5.4. Diatonic Triad Identification

These questions consist of an individual root-position diatonic triad which will either be the **I**, **IV**, **V** or **VI** of the respective key. Please write the chord symbol, followed by the (roman numeral) chord function in parentheses.

Questions 1-6 are in the key of G. Options are:- **G (I)**, **C (IV)**, **D (V)**, or **Emi (VI)**.

1. _____ (   )   4. _____ (   )

2. _____ (   )   5. _____ (   )

3. _____ (   )   6. _____ (   )

Questions 7-12 are in the key of F. Options are:- **F (I)**, **Bb (IV)**, **C (V)**, or **Dmi (VI)**.

7. _____ (   )   10. _____ (   )

8. _____ (   )   11. _____ (   )

9. _____ (   )   12. _____ (   )

(5.4. contd.)

Questions 13-22 consist of melodies to which diatonic triads and bass notes are to be added. Within each key the harmonization options are either the **I**, **IV**, **V** or **VI** diatonic triads. (Refer to Chapter 3 paragraphs **1.2. - 1.4.** if required).

Key of C   13.   14.

15.   16.

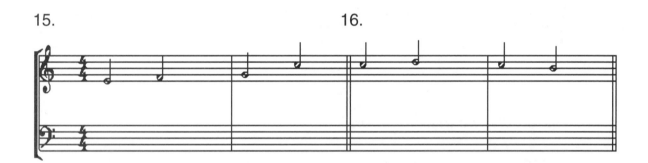

Key of G   17.   18.

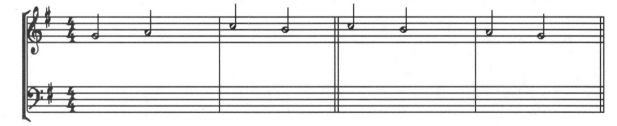

(5.4. contd)

Key of F   19.   20.

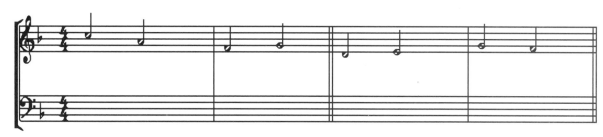

Key of D   21.   22.

Questions 23-34 consist of diatonic triad 'pairs' again limited to the **I**, **IV**, **V** or **VI** diatonic triads of the key. Write your answers (chord symbols) below:

Key of G

23. _____ _____   26. _____ _____

24 _____ _____   27. _____ _____

25. _____ _____   28. _____ _____

Key of F

29. _____ _____   32. _____ _____

30. _____ _____   33. _____ _____

31. _____ _____   34. _____ _____

(5.4. contd)

Questions 35-46 consist of progressions containing 3 triads each, again limited to the **I**, **IV**, **V** or **VI** diatonic triads of the key. Write your answers (chord symbols) be low:

Key of G

35. _____ _____ _____   38. _____ _____ _____
36. _____ _____ _____   39. _____ _____ _____
37. _____ _____ _____   40. _____ _____ _____

Key of F

41. _____ _____ _____   44. _____ _____ _____
42. _____ _____ _____   45. _____ _____ _____
43. _____ _____ _____   46. _____ _____ _____

5.5.   **BASS LINE DICTATION/TRANSCRIPTION**

Write our your answers below:

1.   2.

3.   4.

5.   6.

7.   8.

9.   10.

6. Eartraining Assignments - Workbook Answers

6.1. Melodic Interval Identification answers

(Perfect 4ths and Augmented 4ths)

1.	MI	-	LA	(Per4)	7.	TI	-	FA	(Aug4)
2.	SO	-	DO	(Per4)	8.	RE	-	SO	(Per4)
3.	SO	-	RE	(Per4)	9.	LA	-	RE	(Per4)
4.	FA	-	TI	(Per4)	10.	FA	-	DO	(Per4)
5.	TI	-	MI	(Per4)	11.	LA	-	MI	(Per4)
6.	DO	-	FA	(Per4)	12.	FA	-	TI	(Aug4)

(Perfect 5ths and Diminished 5ths)

13.	DO	-	SO	(Per5)	19.	LA	-	MI	(Per5)
14.	MI	-	TI	(Per5)	20.	TI	-	FA	(Dim5)
15.	LA	-	RE	(Per5)	21.	SO	-	DO	(Per5)
16.	SO	-	RE	(Per5)	22.	RE	-	SO	(Per5)
17.	FA	-	TI	(Dim5)	23.	RE	-	LA	(Per5)
18.	FA	-	DO	(Per5)	24.	TI	-	MI	(Per5)

(6.1. contd.)

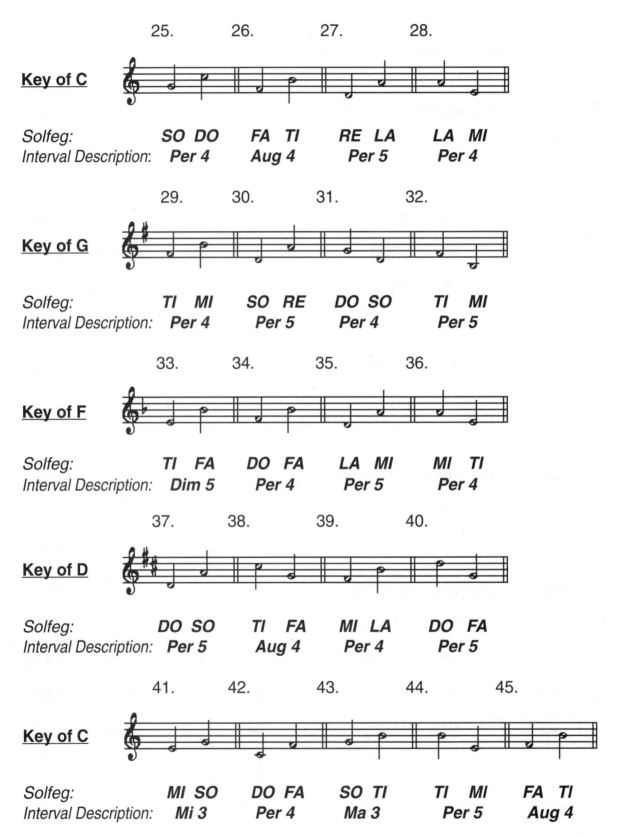

Key of C

Solfeg: **SO DO   FA TI   RE LA   LA MI**
Interval Description: **Per 4   Aug 4   Per 5   Per 4**

Key of G

Solfeg: **TI MI   SO RE   DO SO   TI MI**
Interval Description: **Per 4   Per 5   Per 4   Per 5**

Key of F

Solfeg: **TI FA   DO FA   LA MI   MI TI**
Interval Description: **Dim 5   Per 4   Per 5   Per 4**

Key of D

Solfeg: **DO SO   TI FA   MI LA   DO FA**
Interval Description: **Per 5   Aug 4   Per 4   Per 5**

Key of C

Solfeg: **MI SO   DO FA   SO TI   TI MI   FA TI**
Interval Description: **Mi 3   Per 4   Ma 3   Per 5   Aug 4**

(6.1. contd)

46.   47.   48.   49.   50.

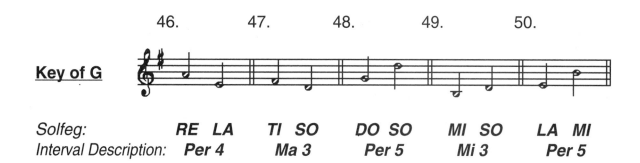

Key of G

Solfeg: **RE LA   TI SO   DO SO   MI SO   LA MI**
Interval Description: **Per 4   Ma 3   Per 5   Mi 3   Per 5**

6.2.   Harmonic Interval Identification answers

(Perfect 4ths and Augmented 4ths)

1.	RE	-	SO	(Per4)	5.	MI	-	LA	(Per4)
2.	TI	-	MI	(Per4)	6.	SO	-	DO	(Per4)
3.	FA	-	TI	(Aug4)	7.	FA	-	TI	(Aug4)
4.	DO	-	FA	(Per4)	8.	LA	-	RE	(Per4)

(Perfect 5ths and Diminished 5ths)

9.	LA	-	MI	(Per5)	13.	SO	-	RE	(Per5)
10.	DO	-	SO	(Per5)	14.	RE	-	LA	(Per5)
11.	MI	-	TI	(Per5)	15.	FA	-	DO	(Per5)
12.	TI	-	FA	(Dim5)	16.	TI	-	FA	(Dim5)

(6.2. contd)

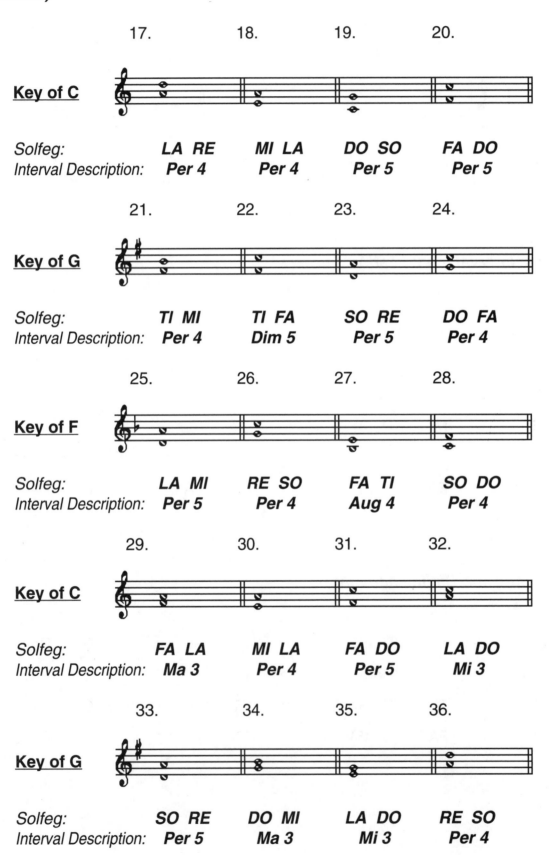

	17.	18.	19.	20.
Key of C				
Solfeg:	**LA RE**	**MI LA**	**DO SO**	**FA DO**
Interval Description:	**Per 4**	**Per 4**	**Per 5**	**Per 5**

	21.	22.	23.	24.
Key of G				
Solfeg:	**TI MI**	**TI FA**	**SO RE**	**DO FA**
Interval Description:	**Per 4**	**Dim 5**	**Per 5**	**Per 4**

	25.	26.	27.	28.
Key of F				
Solfeg:	**LA MI**	**RE SO**	**FA TI**	**SO DO**
Interval Description:	**Per 5**	**Per 4**	**Aug 4**	**Per 4**

	29.	30.	31.	32.
Key of C				
Solfeg:	**FA LA**	**MI LA**	**FA DO**	**LA DO**
Interval Description:	**Ma 3**	**Per 4**	**Per 5**	**Mi 3**

	33.	34.	35.	36.
Key of G				
Solfeg:	**SO RE**	**DO MI**	**LA DO**	**RE SO**
Interval Description:	**Per 5**	**Ma 3**	**Mi 3**	**Per 4**

6.3.   **MELODIC DICTATION/TRANSCRIPTION ANSWERS**

6.4. Diatonic Triad Identification answers

(individual triad recognition)

Key of G

1.	*C*	(IV)	4.	*D*	(V)
2.	*C*	(I)	5.	*Emi*	(VI)
3.	*Emi*	(VI)	6.	*C*	(IV)

Key of F

7.	*F*	(I)	10.	*C*	(V)
8.	*Dmi*	(VI)	11.	*Bb*	(IV)
9.	*Bb*	(IV)	12.	*Dmi*	(VI)

(harmonization questions)

Key of C

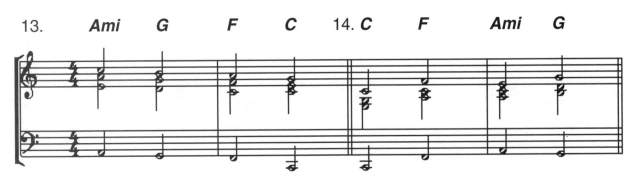

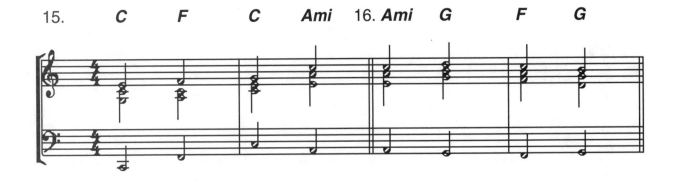

(6.4. contd)

Key of G

17. G D C Emi 18. C G D Emi

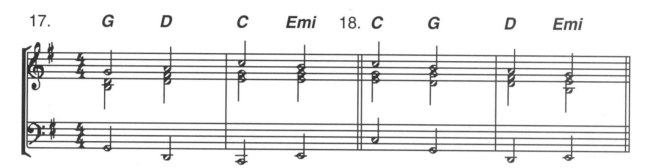

Key of F

19. F Dmi Bb C 20. Dmi C C Bb

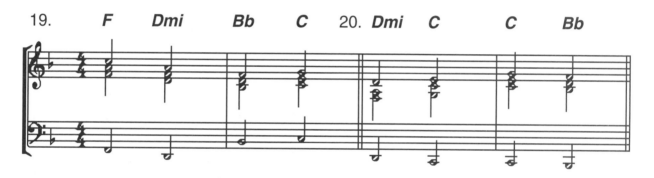

Key of D

21. D G A Bmi 22. A G Bmi D

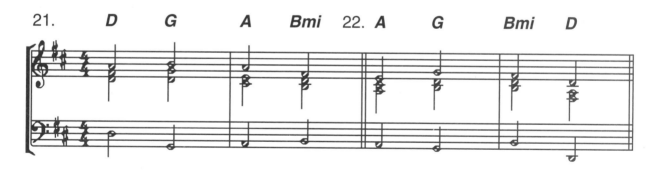

(2-chord progressions)

Key of G

23. G C
24. D G
25. D Emi

26. Emi C
27. C G
28. Emi G

(6.4. contd)

Key of F

29.	**C**	**F**
30.	**Bb**	**C**
31.	**Bb**	**Dmi**

32.	**F**	**Bb**
33.	**Dmi**	**C**
34.	**Dmi**	**F**

(3-chord progressions)

Key of G

35.	**G**	**C**	**D**
36.	**G**	**D**	**Emi**
37.	**Emi**	**C**	**G**

38.	**G**	**Emi**	**D**
39.	**C**	**D**	**G**
40.	**D**	**C**	**Emi**

Key of F

41.	**Bb**	**C**	**F**
42.	**Bb**	**C**	**Dmi**
43.	**Dmi**	**F**	**Bb**

44.	**Bb**	**F**	**C**
45.	**C**	**Dmi**	**F**
46.	**F**	**C**	**Dmi**

6.5.   **BASS LINE DICTATION/TRANSCRIPTION ANSWERS**

Major 2nd/Minor 7th intervals and the III diatonic triad

1.   Theory and Notation

1.1.   Continuing our study of the interval relationships found within a major scale, we will now focus on the diatonic major 2nd and minor 7th intervals. The major 2nd has a span of one whole-step (or 2 half-steps). The minor 7th has a span of 5 whole steps (or 10 half-steps) and is the inversion of the major 2nd interval.

1.2.   These are the melodic major 2nd and minor 7th intervals present within the major scale (keys illustrated are the 3 most recent keys studied - F, D and Bb):-

KEY OF F

Melodic Major 2nds Ascending

DO RE (DO)   RE MI FA SO SO LA (SO)   LA TI (DO)

Melodic Major 2nds Descending

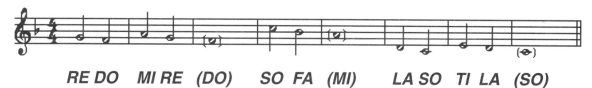

RE DO   MI RE (DO)   SO FA (MI)   LA SO TI LA (SO)

Melodic Minor 7ths Ascending

RE DO   MI RE (DO)   SO FA (MI)   LA SO TI LA (SO)

Melodic Minor 7hs Descending

DO RE (DO)   RE MI FA SO SO   LA (SO)   LA TI (DO)

1 .2. contd.

KEY OF D

Melodic Major 2nds Ascending

DO RE (DO) RE MI FA SO SO LA (SO) LA TI (DO)

Melodic Major 2nds Descending

RE DO MI RE (DO) SO FA (MI) LA SO TI LA (SO)

Melodic Minor 7ths Ascending

RE DO MI RE (DO) SO FA (MI) LA SO TI LA (SO)

Melodic Minor 7ths Descending

DO RE (DO) RE MI FA SO SO LA (SO) LA TI (DO)

KEY OF Bb

Melodic Major 2nds Ascending

DO RE (DO) RE MI FA SO SO LA (SO) LA TI (DO)

Melodic Major 2nds Descending

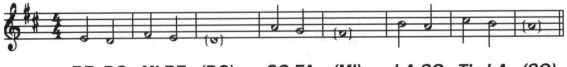

RE DO MI RE (DO) SO FA (MI) LA SO TI LA (SO)

1.2. contd.   <u>**KEY OF Bb (contd)**</u>

Melodic Minor 7ths Ascending

RE DO   MI RE (DO)   SO FA   (MI)   LA SO   TI LA   (SO)

Melodic Minor 7ths Descending

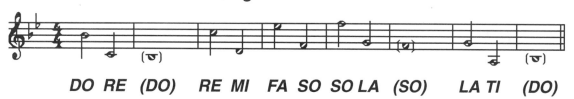

DO RE   (DO)   RE MI   FA SO   SO LA   (SO)   LA TI   (DO)

Again note that when an interval ends on an active tone, the natural resolution is also shown i.e. **DO - RE** to **DO**.

1.3.   These are the harmonic major 2nd and minor 7th intervals present within the major scale (again in the keys of F, D and Bb):-

<u>**KEY OF F**</u>

Harmonic Major 2nds

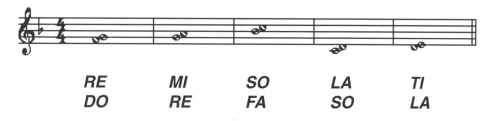

RE	MI	SO	LA	TI
DO	RE	FA	SO	LA

Harmonic Minor 7ths

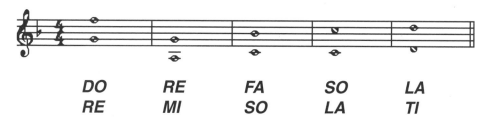

DO	RE	FA	SO	LA
RE	MI	SO	LA	TI

(1.3. contd)

KEY OF D

Harmonic Major 2nds

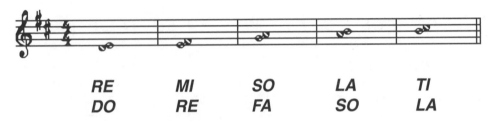

RE	MI	SO	LA	TI
DO	RE	FA	SO	LA

Harmonic Minor 7ths

DO	RE	FA	SO	LA
RE	MI	SO	LA	TI

KEY OF Bb

Harmonic Major 2nds

RE	MI	SO	LA	TI
DO	RE	FA	SO	LA

Harmonic Minor 7ths

DO	RE	FA	SO	LA
RE	MI	SO	LA	TI

1.4. The major 2nd and minor 7th intervals illustrated above, again have different characteristics from the previously discussed diatonic 3rd/6th and 4th/5th intervals. Melodically the Major 2nd interval is frequently encountered, and generally occurs between a resting tone and an adjacent active tone (the exception being the **LA-TI** interval). Although technically a 'symmetric' interval (see root interval discussion in Chapter 5 paragraphs **1.17. - 1.19.**) the Major 2nd nonetheless has a melodic and 'scalewise' impression. Melodically the Minor 7th is a large and angular interval which is less frequently encountered. In a melodic context larger intervals such as Minor 7ths might typically be followed by one or more smaller intervals (i.e. 2nds/3rds) moving in the opposite direction to the larger interval.

1.5. Harmonically both of these intervals (Major 2nd and Minor 7th) will have a 'dissonant' quality, as opposed to the 'consonant' quality of the previously-discussed 3rd/6th and 4th/5th intervals (augmented 4th and diminished 5th excepted). Additionally the Major 2nd has a rather 'clustered' effect due to the smaller interval span.

1.6. All major 2nd and minor 7th intervals will consist of **DO-RE**, **RE-MI**, **FA-SO**, **SO-LA**, or **LA-TI** pairs of notes. In addition to the above-mentioned interval characteristics, there will also be differences in impression due to the respective active & resting qualities:-

DO-RE/ RE-DO **DO** is a resting tone and **RE** is an active tone. Melodically when ending on **RE** (ascending major 2nd/descending minor 7th) the interval will want to resolve to **DO** (or **MI**). When ending on **DO** (ascending minor 7th/descending major 2nd) the interval will not need resolution as we have landed on the resting tone **DO**. However in the case of the ascending **RE-DO** minor 7th interval, this is something of an 'unprepared' resolution as we have not resolved into **DO** via an adjacent active tone.

RE-MI/ MI-RE **RE** is an active tone and **MI** is a resting tone. Melodically when ending on **RE** (ascending minor 7th/descending major 2nd) the interval will want to resolve to **DO**. When ending on **MI** (ascending major 2nd/descending minor 7th) the interval will not need resolution as we have landed on the resting tone **MI**. However in the case of the descending **RE-MI** minor 7th interval, this is something of an 'unprepared' resolution as we have not resolved into **MI** via an adjacent active tone.

FA-SO/ SO-FA **FA** is a active tone and **SO** is a resting tone. Melodically when ending on **FA** (descending major 2nd/ascending minor 7th) the interval will want to resolve to **MI**. When ending on **SO** (ascending major 2nd/descending minor 7th) the interval will not need resolution as we have landed on the resting tone **SO**. However in the case of the descending **FA-SO** minor 7th interval, this is something of an 'unprepared' resolution as we have not resolved into **SO** via an adjacent active tone.

1.6. contd.

SO-LA/
LA-SO
SO is a resting tone and **LA** is an active tone. Melodically when ending on **LA** (ascending major 2nd/descending minor 7th) the interval will want to resolve to **SO** (or up to **DO** via **TI**). When ending on **SO** (ascending minor 7th/descending major 2nd) the interval will not need resolution as we have landed on the resting tone **SO**. However in the case of the ascending **LA-SO** minor 7th interval, this is something of an 'unprepared' resolution as we have not resolved into **SO** via an adjacent active tone.

LA-TI/
TI-LA
Both of these tones are active, creating an active interval. Melodically when ending on **TI** (ascending major 2nd/descending minor 7th) the interval will want to resolve to **DO**. When ending on **LA** (ascending minor 7th/descending major 2nd) the interval will want to resolve to **SO**.

1.7.   Also in this chapter we will discuss some more rhythmic combinations, this time featuring dolled quarter/eighth note groupings. Now we will see single eighth notes (written with a 'tail') as opposed to the previous eighth- note groups which were 'beamed' together. Consider the following new rhythms:

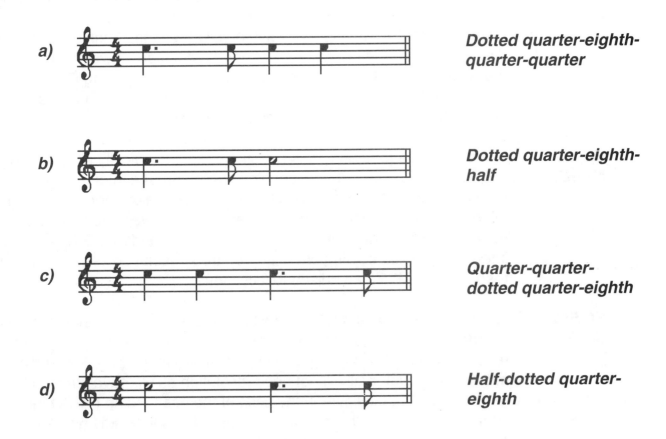

a) **Dotted quarter-eighth-quarter-quarter**

b) **Dotted quarter-eighth-half**

c) **Quarter-quarter-dotted quarter-eighth**

d) **Half-dotted quarter-eighth**

1.8.   In a melodic context these rhythmic patterns might occur as follows:-

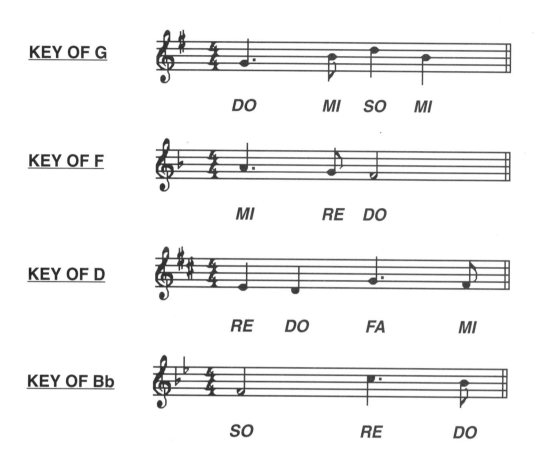

KEY OF G

DO   MI   SO   MI

KEY OF F

MI   RE   DO

KEY OF D

RE   DO   FA   MI

KEY OF Bb

SO   RE   DO

In these contexts the eighth note following the dotted quarter can be thought of as a 'pickup' into a primary beat (either beat **3**, or beat **1** of the following measure). As before, we note that the total number of beats in each measure still adds up to the time signature.

1.9.   Also in this chapter we will continue our work on diatonic triad recognition, by adding the **III minor** triad to the available possibilities as follows (key of C):

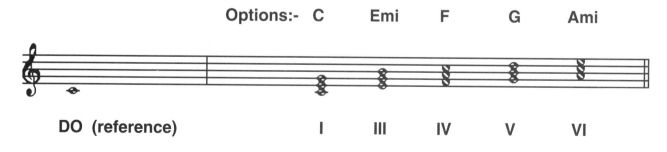

Options:- C   Emi   F   G   Ami

DO (reference)   I   III   IV   V   VI

(Refer to previous text for characteristics of the I, IV, V and VI diatonic triads).

1.10. The **III minor** diatonic triad (containing **MI-SO-TI**) can be recognized as follows:-

CHORD QUALITY - The III triad has the same 'minor' characteristics as the VI minor - refer to Chapter 5 paragraph **1.10.**

ACTIVE/RESTING QUALITIES - The active element in the III triad is **TI**, which wants to resolve up to **DO**. This can give the III triad triad an upward 'pull' or resolution energy. The other tones **MI** and **SO** however are resting tones.

1.11. We will also extend our 'melody harmonization' and 'chord progression' diatonic triad exercises to now include the III minor triad. For the melody harmonization this adds to the 'ear decisions' required, as follows:

DIATONIC MELODY NOTE	DIATONIC TRIAD HARMONIZATION OPTIONS
DO	*I Major* (i.e. **C** in the key of C) *IV Major* (i.e. **F** in the key of C) *VI Minor* (i.e. **Ami** in the key of C)
RE	*V Major* (i.e. **G** in the key of C)
MI	*I Major* (i.e. **C** in the key of C) *III Minor* (i.e. **Emi** in the key of C) *VI Minor* (i.e. **Ami** in the key of C)
FA	*IV Major* (i.e. **F** in the key of C)
SO	*I Major* (i.e. **C** in the key of C) *III Minor* (i.e. **Emi** in the key of C) *V Major* (i.e. **G** in the key of C)
LA	*IV Major* (i.e. **F** in the key of C) *VI Minor* (i.e. **Ami** in the key of C)
TI	*III Minor* (i.e. **Emi** in the key of C) *V Major* (i.e. **G** in the key of C)

As before, we will be combining our sense of diatonic triad 'chord quality' with hearing the active/resting nature of each triad, in order to do these harmonization and progression exercises.

118

2. *Class/Study Activities*

2.1. *Interval singing and recognition*

- Singing drills using major 2nd and minor 7th intervals, in the keys of D and Bb

- Recognition of (melodic and harmonic) all interval types covered so far, in the keys of G, F and D.

2.2. *Melodic dictation/transcription*

- Transcribing melodies containing major 2nd and minor 7th intervals, using all rhythmic combinations covered so far, in the keys of C, G and F.

- Transcribing melodies using simpler rhythms and intervals, in the key of D.

2.3. *Diatonic triad recognition*

- Recognition of **I**, **III**, **IV**, **V** and **VI** diatonic triads in root position, in the keys of F and D.

- Harmonization of (given) 4-note melodies with **I**, **III**, **IV**, **V**, or **VI** diatonic triads, in the keys of C, G, F and D.

- Identifying 2- and 3-chord progressions limited to the **I**, **III**, **IV**, **V**, and **VI** diatonic triads, in the keys of F and D.

2.4. *Bass line dictation/transcription*

- Transcribing bass lines containing whole note, half-note and quarter note rhythms, in the keys of C, G, F and D.

(2.1.) **VOCAL DRILLS - MAJOR 2nd INTERVALS - KEY OF D**

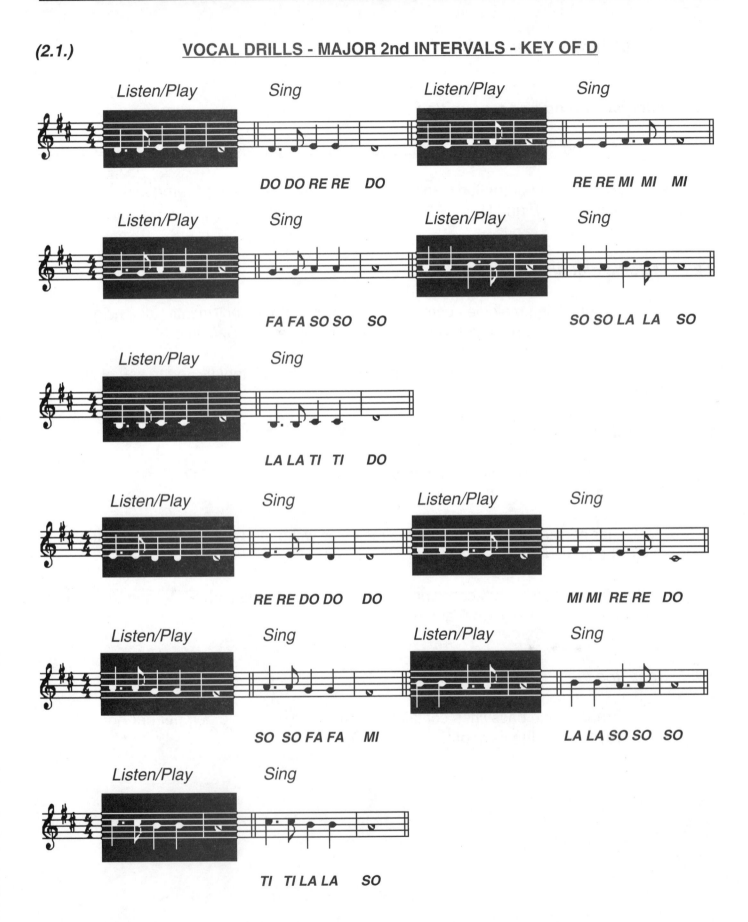

(2.1. contd)   **VOCAL DRILLS - MINOR 7th INTERVALS - KEY OF D**

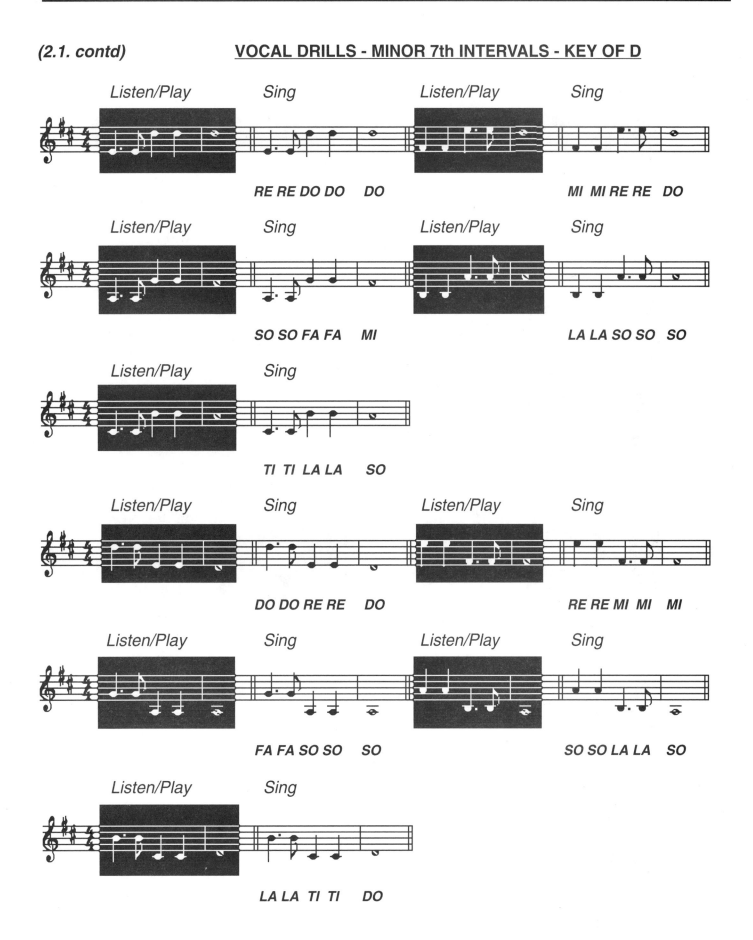

(2.1. contd)   <u>VOCAL DRILLS - MAJOR 2nd INTERVALS - KEY OF Bb</u>

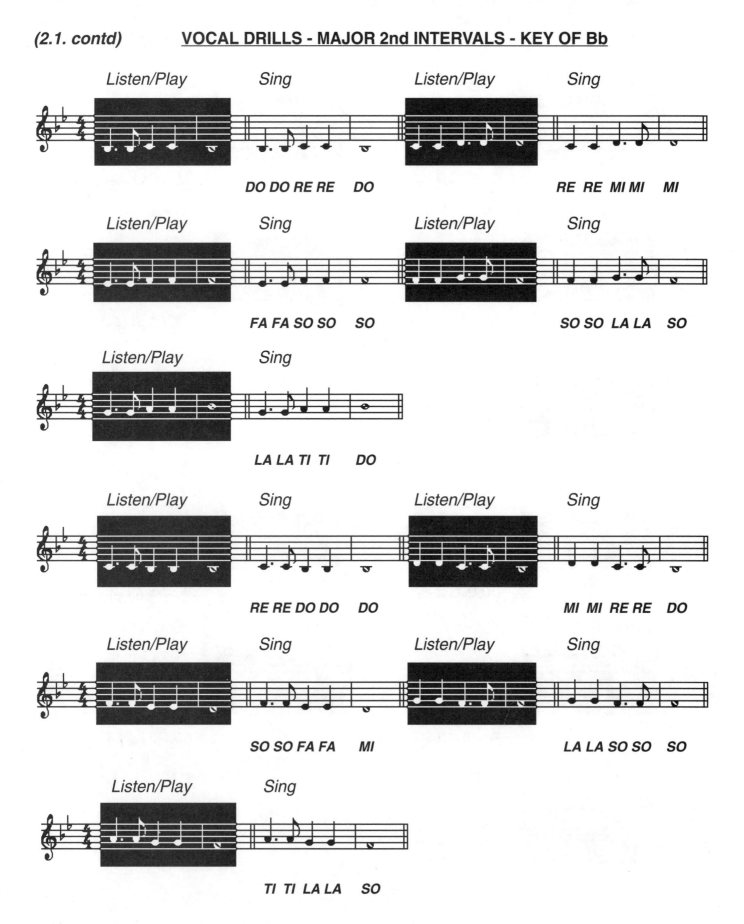

(2.1. contd)   **VOCAL DRILLS - MINOR 7th INTERVALS - KEY OF Bb**

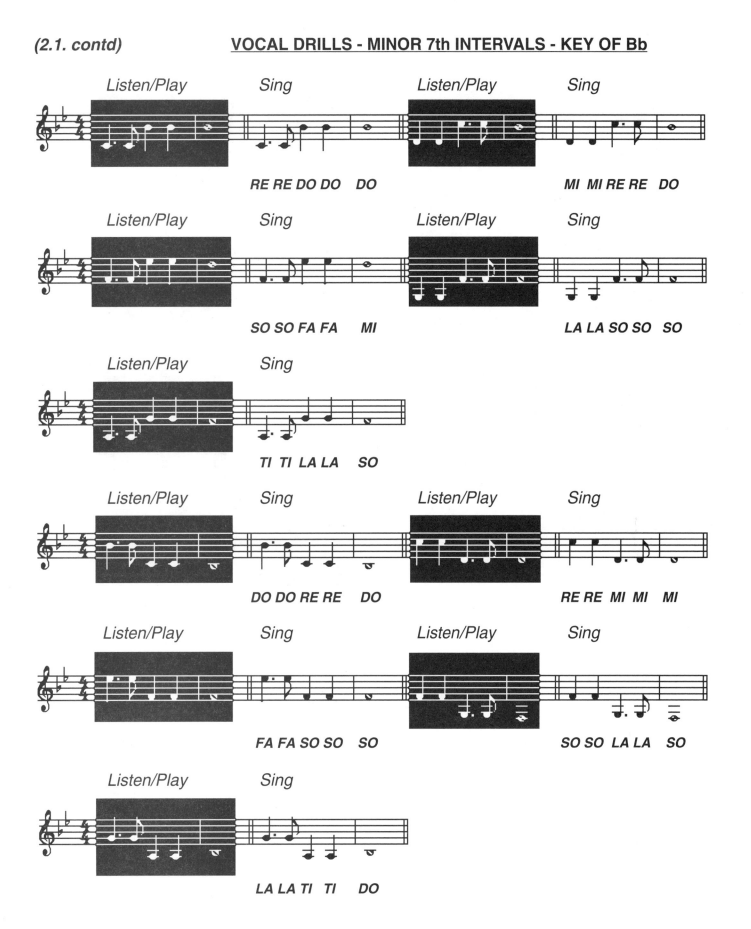

RE RE DO DO DO

MI MI RE RE DO

SO SO FA FA   MI

LA LA SO SO SO

TI TI LA LA   SO

DO DO RE RE   DO

RE RE MI MI MI

FA FA SO SO SO

SO SO LA LA   SO

LA LA TI TI   DO

CHAPTER SIX

MELODIES FOR SINGING AND TRANSCRIPTION

(2.2. contd)   <u>MELODIES FOR SINGING AND TRANSCRIPTION (contd)</u>

3. Theory Assignments

3.1. Supplementary worksheets
- keys of **C** (p193), **G** (p199), **F** (p205), **D** (p211) and **Bb** (p217).

- Write out notes on treble clef staff corresponding to the major 2nd and minor 7th melodic (ascending and descending) and harmonic intervals.
- Write out notes on treble and bass clef staffs corresponding to the **III minor** diatonic triad.

4. Eartraining Tapes Available (see page iv) - tape contents for this chapter

4.1. The Eartraining tape available for Chapter 6 consists of the following:-

- melodic interval identification questions (major 2nds/minor 7ths) ascending and descending
  - you may fill out your answers in section **5.1.**
  - you may check against correct answers in section **6.1.**

- harmonic interval identification questions (major 2nds/minor 7ths)
  - you may fill out your answers in section **5.2.**
  - you may check against correct answers in section **6.2.**

- melodic dictation/transcription questions
  - you may fill out your answers in section **5.3.**
  - you may check against correct answers in section **6.3.**

- diatonic triad recognition (individual triads, harmonizing 4-note melodies, and 2- and 3-chord progressions)
  - you may fill out your answers in section **5.4.**
  - you may check against correct answers in section **6.4.**

- bass line dictation/transcription
  - you may fill out your answers in section **5.5.**
  - you may check against correct answers in section **6.5.**

5.   Eartraining Assignments - Workbook Questions

(fill out your answers here)

5.1.   Melodic Interval Identification

Questions 1-12 consist of major 2nd intervals ascending or descending. The options are:-

DO-RE, **RE-MI**, **FA-SO**, **SO-LA**, **LA-TI** (ascending),or
RE-DO, **MI-RE**, **SO-FA**, **LA-SO**, **TI-LA** (descending).

Write your (solfeg) answers below:-

1.   _____ _____   7.   _____ _____
2.   _____ _____   8.   _____ _____
3.   _____ _____   9.   _____ _____
4.   _____ _____   10.   _____ _____
5.   _____ _____   11.   _____ _____
6.   _____ _____   12.   _____ _____

Questions 13-24 consist of minor 7th intervals ascending or descending. The options are:-

RE-DO, **MI-RE**, **SO-FA**, **LA-SO**, **TI-LA** (ascending),or
DO-RE, **RE-MI**, **FA-SO**, **SO-LA**, **LA-TI** (descending).

Write your (solfeg) answers below:-

13.   _____ _____   19.   _____ _____
14.   _____ _____   20.   _____ _____
15.   _____ _____   21.   _____ _____
16.   _____ _____   22.   _____ _____
17.   _____ _____   23.   _____ _____
18.   _____ _____   24.   _____ _____

(5.1. contd)

Questions 25-40 now comprise all of the above interval possibilities (i.e. major 2nds and minor 7ths, ascending and descending). For each question, write the notes on the staff, together with the solfeg and interval description.

25.   26.   27.   28.

Key of G

Solfeg:
Interval Description:

29.   30.   31.   32.

Key of F

Solfeg:
Interval Description:

33.   34.   35.   36.

Key of D

Solfeg:
Interval Description:

37.   38.   39.   40.

Key of Bb

Solfeg:
Interval Description:

(Questions 41-50 now include all intervals studied prior to this week's lesson, within the range of possibilities).

(5.1. contd)

41.   42.   43.   44.   45.

Key of G

Solfeg: _____ _____   _____ _____   _____ _____   _____ _____   _____ _____
Interval Description: _____   _____   _____   _____   _____

46.   47.   48.   49.   50.

Key of F

Solfeg: _____ _____   _____ _____   _____ _____   _____ _____   _____ _____
Interval Description: _____   _____   _____   _____   _____

5.2. *Harmonic Interval Identification*

Questions 1-8 consist of major 2nd intervals played harmonically i.e. both tones played simultaneously. The options are **DO-RE**, **RE-MI**, **FA-SO**, **SO-LA**, or **LA-TI**.

Write your (solfeg) answers below:-

1.   _____ _____   5.   _____ _____
2.   _____ _____   6.   _____ _____
3.   _____ _____   7.   _____ _____
4.   _____ _____   8.   _____ _____

Questions 9-16 consist of minor 7th intervals played harmonically. The options are **RE-DO**, **MI-RE**, **SO-FA**, **LA-SO**, or **TI-LA**.

Write your (solfeg) answers below:-

9.   _____ _____   13.   _____ _____
10.   _____ _____   14.   _____ _____
11.   _____ _____   15.   _____ _____
12.   _____ _____   16.   _____ _____

(5.2. contd)

Questions 17-28 now comprise all of the above interval possibilities (i.e. harmonic major 2nd and minor 7th intervals). For each question, write the notes on the staff, together with the solfeg and interval description.

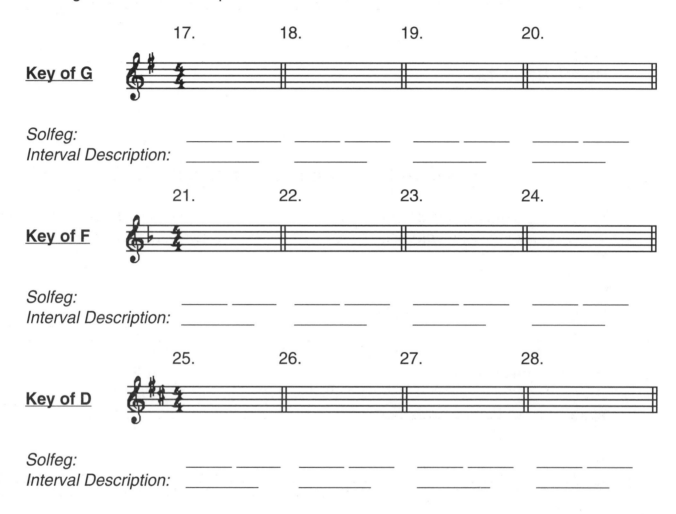

Key of G

Solfeg:
Interval Description:

Key of F

Solfeg:
Interval Description:

Key of D

Solfeg:
Interval Description:

(Questions 29-36 now include all intervals studied prior to this week's lesson, within the range of possibilities).

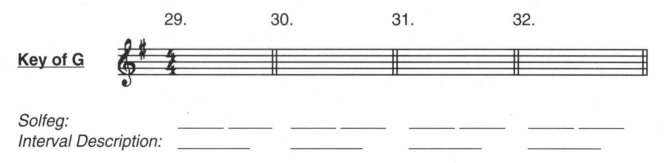

Key of G

Solfeg:
Interval Description:

(5.2. contd)

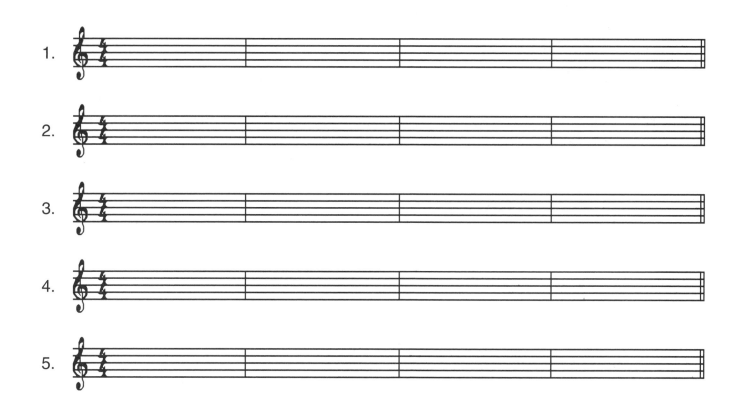

33.   34.   35.   36.

Key of F

Solfeg:
Interval Description:

5.3.   MELODIC DICTATION/TRANSCRIPTION

These 10 questions consist of melodies based on this chapter's material. *Listen for the new major 2nd and minor 7th intervals being used.* Write your answers below:-

1.

2.

3.

4.

5.

(5.3. contd)

6.

7.

8.

9.

10.

5.4. Diatonic Triad Identification

These questions consist of an individual root-position diatonic triad which will either be the **I**, **III**, **IV**, **V** or **VI** of the respective key. Please write the chord symbol, followed by the (roman numeral) chord function in parentheses.

Questions 1-6 are in the key of F.
Options are:- **F (I)**, **Ami (III)**, **Bb (IV)**, **C (V)**, or **Dmi (VI)**.

1.	_____ ( )	4.	_____ ( )
2.	_____ ( )	5.	_____ ( )
3.	_____ ( )	6.	_____ ( )

Questions 7-12 are in the key of D.
Options are:- **D (I)**, **F#mi (III)**, **G (IV)**, **A (V)**, or **Bmi (VI)**.

7.	_____ ( )	10.	_____ ( )
8.	_____ ( )	11.	_____ ( )
9.	_____ ( )	12.	_____ ( )

(5.4. contd)

Questions 13-22 consist of melodies to which diatonic triads and bass notes are to be added. Within each key the harmonization options are either the **I**, **III**, **IV**, **V** , or **VI** diatonic triads.

(5.4. contd)

Key of D   21.   22.

Questions 23-34 consist of diatonic triad 'pairs' again limited to the **I**, **III**, **IV**, **V**, or **VI** diatonic triads of the key. Write your answers (chord symbols) below:-

Key of F

23. _____ _____   26. _____ _____
24 _____ _____   27. _____ _____
25. _____ _____   28. _____ _____

Key of D

29. _____ _____   32. _____ _____
30. _____ _____   33. _____ _____
31. _____ _____   34. _____ _____

Questions 35-46 consist of progressions containing 3 triads each, again limited to the **I**, **III**, **IV**, **V**, or **VI** diatonic triads of the key. Write your answers (chord symbols) below:-

Key of F

35. _____ _____ _____   38. _____ _____ _____
36. _____ _____ _____   39. _____ _____ _____
37. _____ _____ _____   40. _____ _____ _____

Key of D

41. _____ _____ _____   44. _____ _____ _____
42. _____ _____ _____   45. _____ _____ _____
43. _____ _____ _____   46. _____ _____ _____

5.5.   **BASS LINE DICTATION/TRANSCRIPTION**

Write our your answers below:-

1.   2.

3.   4.

5.   6.

7.   8.

9.   10.

135

6. Eartraining Assignments - Workbook Answers

6.1. Melodic Interval Identification answers

(Major 2nds)

1.	SO	-	LA	7.	RE	-	DO
2.	DO	-	RE	8.	RE	-	MI
3.	MI	-	RE	9.	LA	-	SO
4.	FA	-	SO	10.	DO	-	RE
5.	LA	-	TI	11.	TI	-	LA
6.	SO	-	FA	12.	MI	-	RE

(Minor 7ths)

13.	RE	-	DO	19.	TI	-	LA
14.	SO	-	LA	20.	RE	-	MI
15.	LA	-	TI	21.	LA	-	SO
16.	MI	-	RE	22.	RE	-	DO
17.	SO	-	FA	23.	SO	-	FA
18.	DO	-	RE	24.	SO	-	LA

	25.	26.	27.	28.

Key of G

Solfeg: **RE MI   LA SO   SO FA   RE MI**
Interval Description: **Ma2   Ma2   Mi7   Mi7**

(6.1. contd)

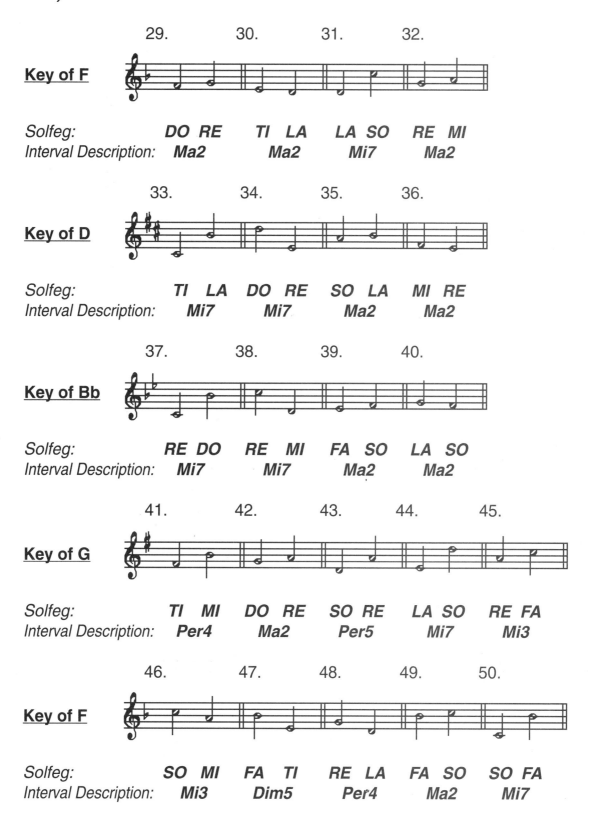

Key of F

Solfeg: **DO RE   TI LA   LA SO   RE MI**
Interval Description: **Ma2   Ma2   Mi7   Ma2**

Key of D

Solfeg: **TI   LA   DO RE   SO LA   MI RE**
Interval Description: **Mi7   Mi7   Ma2   Ma2**

Key of Bb

Solfeg: **RE DO   RE MI   FA SO   LA SO**
Interval Description: **Mi7   Mi7   Ma2   Ma2**

Key of G

Solfeg: **TI MI   DO RE   SO RE   LA SO   RE FA**
Interval Description: **Per4   Ma2   Per5   Mi7   Mi3**

Key of F

Solfeg: **SO MI   FA TI   RE LA   FA SO   SO FA**
Interval Description: **Mi3   Dim5   Per4   Ma2   Mi7**

6.2. Harmonic Interval Identification answers

(Major 2nds)

1.	RE	-	MI	5.	SO	-	LA
2.	LA	-	TI	6.	DO	-	RE
3.	DO	-	RE	7.	FA	-	SO
4.	FA	-	SO	8.	RE	-	MI

(Minor 7ths)

9.	MI	-	RE	13.	TI	-	LA
10.	LA	-	SO	14.	LA	-	SO
11.	RE	-	DO	15.	MI	-	RE
12.	SO	-	FA	16.	SO	-	FA

(6.2. contd)

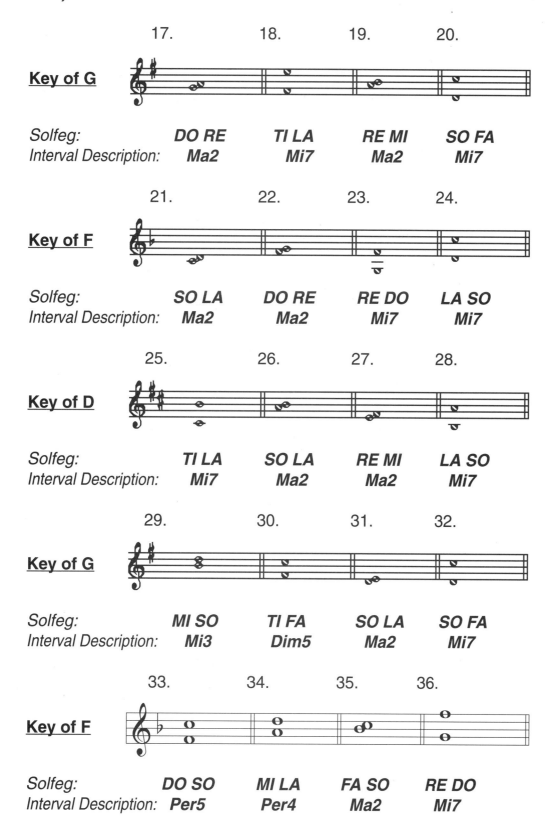

Key of G

	17.	18.	19.	20.
Solfeg:	DO RE	TI LA	RE MI	SO FA
Interval Description:	Ma2	Mi7	Ma2	Mi7

Key of F

	21.	22.	23.	24.
Solfeg:	SO LA	DO RE	RE DO	LA SO
Interval Description:	Ma2	Ma2	Mi7	Mi7

Key of D

	25.	26.	27.	28.
Solfeg:	TI LA	SO LA	RE MI	LA SO
Interval Description:	Mi7	Ma2	Ma2	Mi7

Key of G

	29.	30.	31.	32.
Solfeg:	MI SO	TI FA	SO LA	SO FA
Interval Description:	Mi3	Dim5	Ma2	Mi7

Key of F

	33.	34.	35.	36.
Solfeg:	DO SO	MI LA	FA SO	RE DO
Interval Description:	Per5	Per4	Ma2	Mi7

6.3. **MELODIC DICTATION/TRANSCRIPTION ANSWERS**

6.4. Diatonic Triad Identification answers

(individual triad recognition)

Key of F

1.	*C*	(V)		4.	*F*	(I)
2.	*Ami*	(III)		5.	*Bb*	(IV)
3.	*Dmi*	(VI)		6.	*Ami*	(III)

Key of D

7.	*G*	(IV)		10.	*A*	(V)
8.	*D*	(I)		11.	*Bmi*	(VI)
9.	*F#mi*	(III)		12.	*G*	(IV)

(harmonization questions)

Key of C

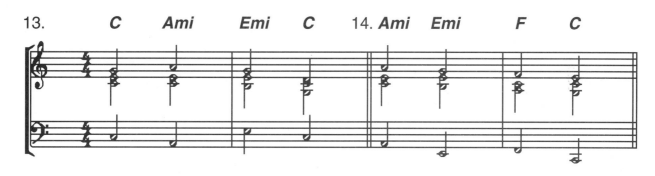

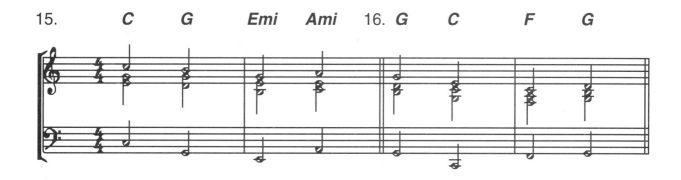

(6.4. contd)

Key of G

17.   **Bmi**   **D**   **G**   **Bmi**   18. **C**   **Bmi**   **D**   **Emi**

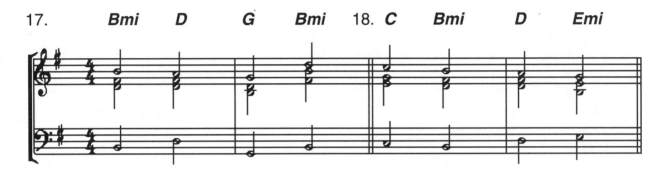

Key of F

19.   **F**   **C**   **Bb**   **Dmi**   20. **Bb**   **C**   **Ami**   **Dmi**

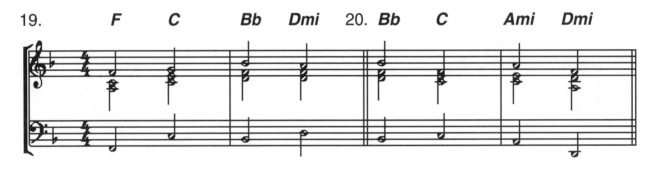

Key of D

21.   **A**   **D**   **A**   **F#mi** 22. **D**   **G**   **F#mi**   **Bmi**

(6.4. contd)

(2-chord progressions)

Key of F

23.	*F*	*Dmi*
24.	*F*	*Bb*
25.	*Bb*	*C*

26.	*F*	*Ami*
27.	*Ami*	*Dmi*
28.	*C*	*F*

Key of D

29.	*D*	*G*
30.	*D*	*Bmi*
31.	*F#mi*	*A*

32.	*A*	*Bmi*
33.	*A*	*D*
34.	*G*	*F#mi*

(3-chord progressions)

Key of F

35.	*F*	*C*	*Dmi*
36.	*F*	*Ami*	*Bb*
37.	*Dmi*	*C*	*Bb*

38.	*Ami*	*F*	*Dmi*
39.	*Bb*	*F*	*Ami*
40.	*Dmi*	*Ami*	*F*

Key of D

41.	*D*	*G*	*A*
42.	*Bmi*	*D*	*G*
43.	*F#mi*	*Bmi*	*G*

44.	*D*	*Bmi*	*A*
45.	*A*	*D*	*F#mi*
46.	*G*	*A*	*Bmi*

6.5.   **BASS LINE DICTATION/TRANSCRIPTION ANSWERS**

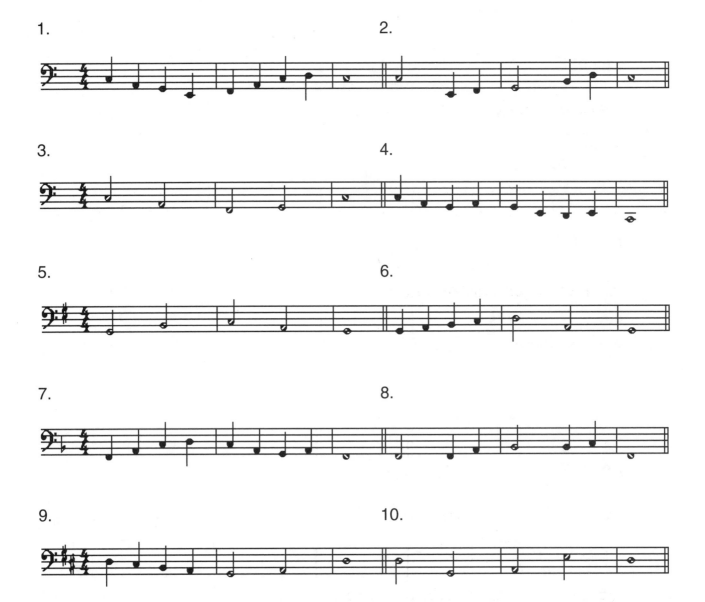

Minor 2nd/Major 7th intervals and the II diatonic triad

1. Theory and Notation

1.1. Continuing our study of the interval relationships found within a major scale, we will now focus on the diatonic minor 2nd and major 7th intervals. The minor 2nd has a span of one half-step. The major 7th has a span of five-and-a-half steps (or 11 half-steps) and is the inversion of the minor 2nd interval.

1.2. These are the melodic minor 2nd and major 7th intervals present within the major scale (keys illustrated are the 3 most recent keys studied - F, D and Bb):-

KEY OF F

Melodic Minor 2nds Ascending

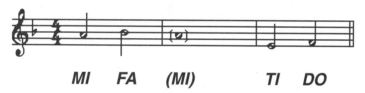

MI   FA   (MI)   TI   DO

Melodic Minor 2nds Descending

FA   MI   DO   TI   (DO)

Melodic Major 7ths Ascending

DO   TI   (DO)   FA   MI

Melodic Major 7ths Descending

TI   DO   MI   FA   (MI)

1.2. contd.

<u>KEY OF D</u>

Melodic Minor 2nds Ascending

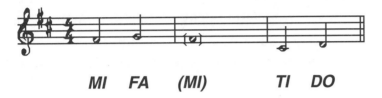

MI   FA   (MI)   TI   DO

Melodic Minor 2nds Descending

FA   MI   DO   TI   (DO)

Melodic Major 7ths Ascending

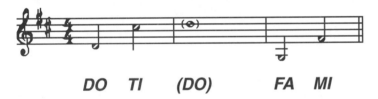

DO   TI   (DO)   FA   MI

Melodic Major 7ths Descending

TI   DO   MI   FA   (MI)

<u>KEY OF Bb</u>

Melodic Minor 2nds Ascending

MI   FA   (MI)   TI   DO

1.2. contd.   <u>**KEY OF Bb (contd)**</u>

Melodic Minor 2nds Descending

FA   MI   DO   TI   (DO)

Melodic Major 7ths Ascending

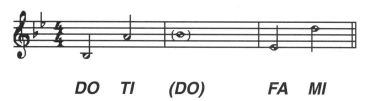

DO   TI   (DO)   FA   MI

Melodic Major 7ths Descending

TI   DO   MI   FA   (MI)

Again note that when an interval ends on an active tone, the natural resolution is also shown i.e. **MI - FA** to **MI**.

1.3.   These are the harmonic minor 2nd and major 7th intervals present within the major scale (keys of F, D and Bb):-

<u>**KEY OF F**</u>

Harmonic Minor 2nds

FA   DO
MI   TI

1.3. contd.   **KEY OF F (contd)**

Harmonic Major 7ths

            TI   MI
            DO   FA

                                        KEY OF D

Harmonic Minor 2nds

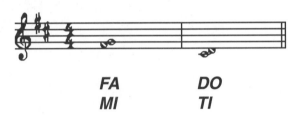

            FA   DO
            MI   TI

Harmonic Major 7ths

            TI   MI
            DO   FA

                                        KEY OF Bb

Harmonic Minor 2nds

            FA   DO
            MI   TI

Harmonic Major 7ths

            TI   MI
            DO   FA

1.4.　　The minor 2nd and major 7th intervals illustrated above will have some characteristics in common with the previously discussed diatonic major 2nd and minor 7th intervals (see Chapter 6 paragraph **1.4.**). Melodically the leading and 'tonal' Minor 2nd interval will have a 'definitive' impression, as it will always be between an active half-step (**TI** or **FA**) and an adjacent resting tone (**DO** or **MI**). Melodically the Major 7th is a large and angular interval which is less frequently encountered (see previous comments regarding Minor 7ths).

1.5.　　Harmonically both of these intervals (Minor 2nd and Major 7th) will have a very dissonant quality - these harmonic intervals are the most dissonant available within a major scale. Additionally with this pair of intervals, there is the largest difference in 'span' between the minor 2nd and (it's inversion) the major 7th.

1.6.　　All minor 2nd and major 7th intervals will consist of either **MI-FA** or **TI-DO** pairs of notes. In addition to the above mentioned interval characteristics, there will also be differences in impression due to the respective active & resting qualities-:

MI-FA/ ***FA-MI***	**MI** is a resting tone and **FA** is an active tone. Melodically when ending on **FA** (ascending minor 2nd/descending major 7th) the interval will want to resolve to **MI**. When ending on **MI** (descending minor 2nd/ ascending major 7th) the interval will not need resolution as we have landed on the resting tone **MI**. However in the case of the ascending **FA-MI** major 7th interval, this is something of an 'unprepared' resolution as we have not resolved into **MI** via an adjacent active tone.
TI-DO/ ***DO-TI***	**DO** is a resting tone and **TI** is an active tone. Melodically when ending on **TI** (ascending major 7th/descending minor 2nd) the interval will want to resolve to **DO**. When ending on **DO** (ascending minor 2nd/descending major 7th) the interval will not need resolution as we have landed on the resting tone **DO**. However in the case of the descending **TI-DO** major 7th interval, this is something of an 'unprepared' resolution as we have not resolved into **DO** via an adjacent active tone.

1.7.　　Also in this chapter we will discuss some more rhythmic combinations, this time featuring anticipations of beat 3 by an eighth-note. Consider the following new rhythms:-

a)　

Eighth-eighth-eighth-eighth tied to a half

1.7. contd.

b)   *Quarter-eighth-eighth tied to a half*

c)   *Dotted quarter-eighth tied to a half*

1.8.   In a melodic context these rhythmic patterns might occur as follows:-

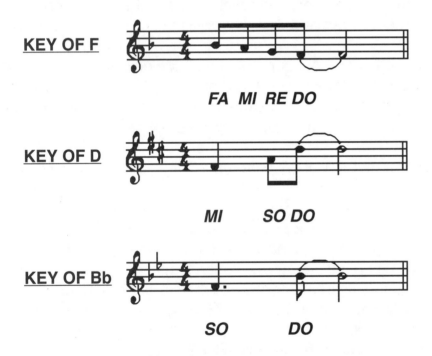

KEY OF F   *FA MI RE DO*

KEY OF D   *MI   SO DO*

KEY OF Bb   *SO   DO*

In these contexts the tied eighth note functions as an anticipation of beat **3** (the second primary beat in a **4/4** measure).

1.9.   Also in this chapter we will continue our work on diatonic triad recognition, by adding the **II minor** triad to the available possibilities as follows (key of C):-

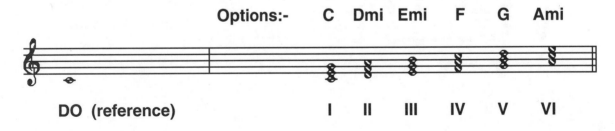

Options:-   C   Dmi   Emi   F   G   Ami

DO (reference)   I   II   III   IV   V   VI

1.9. contd.

(Refer to previous text for characteristics of the **I**, **III**, **IV**, **V** and **VI** triads).

1.10. The **II minor** diatonic triad (containing **RE-FA-LA**) can be recognized as follows:-

CHORD QUALITY - The II triad has the same 'minor' characteristics as the III and VI triads - refer to Chapter 5 text paragraph **1.10.**

ACTIVE/RESTING
QUALITIES - The main active element in the II triad is **FA**, which wants to resolve down to **MI**. Also the other active tones **RE** and **LA** would typically resolve down to **DO** and **SO** respectively. This can give the II triad a downward 'pull' or resolution energy.

1.11. We will also extend our 'melody harmonization' and 'chord progression' diatonic triad exercises to now include the II minor triad. For the melody harmonization, this now adds to the 'ear decisions' required, as follows:-

DIATONIC MELODY NOTE	DIATONIC TRIAD HARMONIZATION OPTIONS
DO	*I Major* (i.e. **C** in the key of C) *IV Major* (i.e. **F** in the key of C) *VI Minor* (i.e. **Ami** in the key of C)
RE	*II Minor* (i.e. **Dmi** in the key of C) *V Major* (i.e. **G** in the key of C)
MI	*I Major* (i.e. **C** in the key of C) *III Minor* (i.e. **Emi** in the key of C) *VI Minor* (i.e. **Ami** in the key of C)
FA	*II Minor* (i.e. **Dmi** in the key of C) *IV Major* (i.e. **F** in the key of C)
SO	*I Major* (i.e. **C** in the key of C) *III Minor* (i.e. **Emi** in the key of C) *V Major* (i.e. **G** in the key of C)

(contd over>>>)

1.11. contd.

DIATONIC MELODY NOTE	DIATONIC TRIAD HARMONIZATION OPTIONS
LA	*II Minor* (i.e. **Dmi** in the key of C) *IV Major* (i.e. **F** in the key of C) *VI Minor* (i.e. **Ami** in the key of C)
TI	*III Minor* (i.e. **Emi** in the key of C) *V Major* (i.e. **G** in the key of C)

As before, we will be combining our sense of diatonic triad 'chord quality' with hearing the active/resting nature of each triad, in order to do these harmonization and progression exercises.

2. Class/Study Activities

2.1. Interval singing and recognition

- Singing drills using minor 2nd and major 7th intervals, in the keys of D and Bb.
- Recognition of (melodic and harmonic) all interval types covered so far, in the keys of G, F and D.

2.2. Melodic dictation/transcription

- Transcribing melodies containing minor 2nd and major 7th intervals, using all rhythmic combinations covered so far, in the keys of C, G, F and D.
- Transcribing melodies using simpler rhythms and intervals, in the key of Bb.

2.3. Diatonic triad recognition

- Recognition of **I**, **II**, **III**, **IV**, **V** and **VI** diatonic triads in root position, in the keys of D and Bb.
- Harmonization of (given) 4-note melodies with **I**, **II**, **III**, **IV**, **V** and **VI** diatonic triads, in the keys of C, G, F, D and Bb.
- Identifying 2- and 3-chord progressions using the **I**, **II**, **III**, **IV**, **V** or **VI** diatonic triads, in the keys of D and Bb.

2.4. Bass line dictation/transcription

- Transcribing bass lines containing all rhythmic combinations covered so far, in the keys of C, G, F, D and Bb.

(2.1.) **VOCAL DRILLS - MINOR 2nd INTERVALS - KEY OF D**

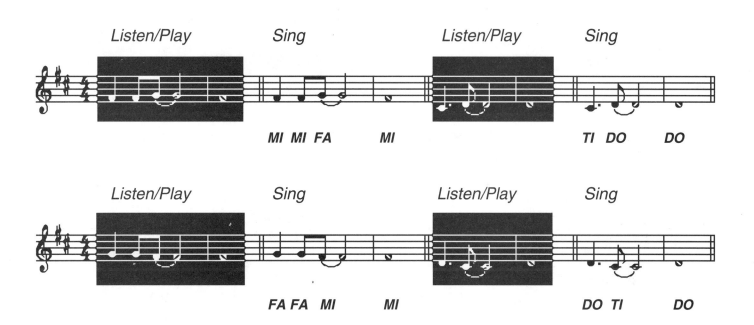

VOCAL DRILLS - MAJOR 7th INTERVALS - KEY OF D

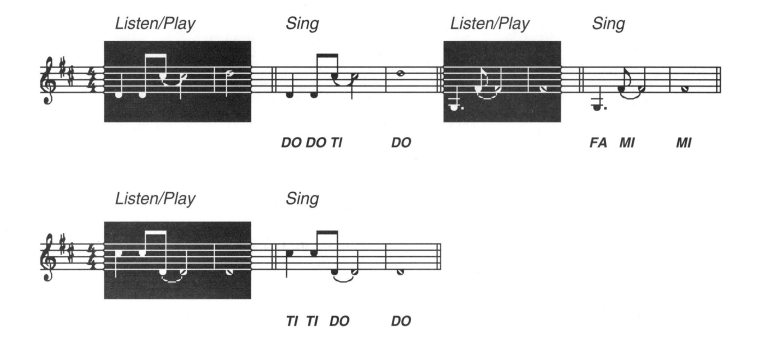

(2.1. contd)   <u>**VOCAL DRILLS - MINOR 2nd INTERVALS - KEY OF Bb**</u>

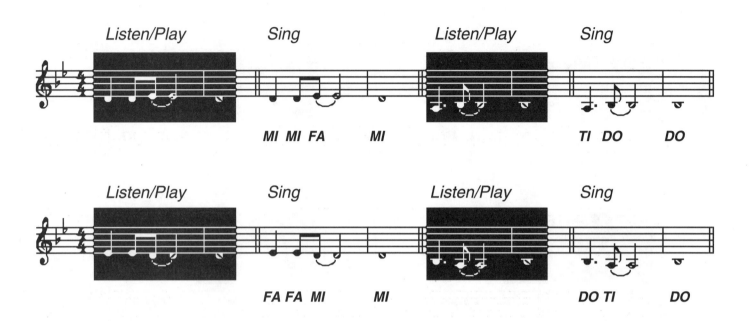

<u>VOCAL DRILLS - MAJOR 7th INTERVALS - KEY OF Bb</u>

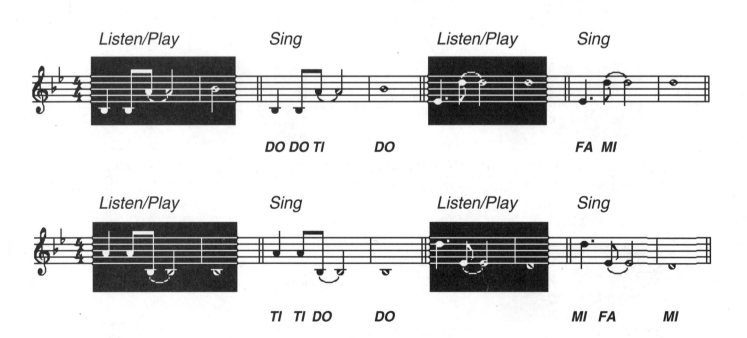

(2.2.)   **MELODIES FOR SINGING AND TRANSCRIPTION**

(2.2. contd)   <u>**MELODIES FOR SINGING AND TRANSCRIPTION (contd)**</u>

3. Theory Assignments

3.1. Supplementary worksheets
- **keys of C** (p193), **G** (p199), **F** (p205), **D** (p211), and **Bb** (p217).

- Write out notes on treble clef staff corresponding to the minor 2nd and major 7th melodic (ascending and descending) and harmonic intervals.
- Write out notes on treble and bass clef staffs corresponding to the **II minor** diatonic triad.

4. Eartraining Tapes Available (see page iv) - tape contents for this chapter

4.1. The Eartraining tape available for Chapter 7 consists of the following:-

- melodic interval identification questions (minor 2nds/major 7ths) ascending and descending
  - you may fill out your answers in section **5.1.**
  - you may check against correct answers in section **6.1.**

- harmonic interval identification questions (minor 2nds/major 7ths)
  - you may fill out your answers in section **5.2.**
  - you may check against correct answers printed in section **6.2.**

- melodic dictation/transcription questions
  - you may fill out your answers in section **5.3.**
  - you may check against correct answers in section **6.3.**

- diatonic triad recognition (individual triads, harmonizing 4-note melodies, and 2- and 3-chord progressions)
  - you may fill out your answers in section **5.4.**
  - you may check against correct answers in section **6.4.**

- bass line dictation/transcription
  - you may fill out your answers in section **5.5.**
  - you may check against correct answers in section **6.5.**

5. _Eartraining Assignments - Workbook Questions_

(fill out your answers here)

5.1. _Melodic Interval Identification_

Questions 1-12 consist of minor 2nd intervals ascending or descending. The options are **MI-FA**, **TI-DO** (ascending) or **FA-MI**, **DO-TI** (descending).

Write your (solfeg) answers below:-

1. _____ _____
2. _____ _____
3. _____ _____
4. _____ _____
5. _____ _____
6. _____ _____

6. _____ _____
7. _____ _____
8. _____ _____
9. _____ _____
10. _____ _____
12. _____ _____

Questions 13-24 consist of major 7th intervals ascending or descending. The options are **DO-TI**, **FA-MI** (ascending) or **TI-DO**, **MI-FA** (descending).

Write your (solfeg) answers below:-

13. _____ _____
14. _____ _____
15. _____ _____
16. _____ _____
17. _____ _____
18. _____ _____

19. _____ _____
20. _____ _____
21. _____ _____
22. _____ _____
23. _____ _____
24. _____ _____

Questions 25-40 now comprise all of the above interval possibilities (i.e. minor 2nds and major 7ths ascending and descending). For each question, write the notes on the staff, together with the solfeg and interval description.

(5.1. contd)

	25.	26.	27.	28.

Key of G

Solfeg: ___ ___   ___ ___   ___ ___   ___ ___
Interval Description: _____   _____   _____   _____

	29.	30.	31.	32.

Key of F

Solfeg: ___ ___   ___ ___   ___ ___   ___ ___
Interval Description: _____   _____   _____   _____

	33.	34.	35.	36.

Key of D

Solfeg: ___ ___   ___ ___   ___ ___   ___ ___
Interval Description: _____   _____   _____   _____

	37.	38.	39.	40.

Key of Bb

Solfeg: ___ ___   ___ ___   ___ ___   ___ ___
Interval Description: _____   _____   _____   _____

(Questions 41-50 now include all intervals studied prior to this chapter, within the range of possibilities).

	41.	42.	43.	44.	45.

Key of F

Solfeg: ___ ___   ___ ___   ___ ___   ___ ___   ___ ___
Interval Description: _____   _____   _____   _____

(5.1. contd.)

| 46. | 47. | 48. | 49. | 50. |

Key of D

Solfeg:
Interval Description:

5.2. Harmonic Interval Identification

Questions 1-8 consist of minor 2nd intervals played harmonically i.e. both tones played simultaneously. The options are **MI-FA** or **TI-DO**.

Write your (solfeg) answers below:-

1. _____ _____   5. _____ _____
2. _____ _____   6. _____ _____
3. _____ _____   7. _____ _____
4. _____ _____   8. _____ _____

Questions 9-16 consist of major 7th intervals played harmonically. The options are **DO-TI** or **FA-MI**.

Write your (solfeg) answers below:-

9. _____ _____   13. _____ _____
10. _____ _____   14. _____ _____
11. _____ _____   15. _____ _____
12. _____ _____   16. _____ _____

(5.2. contd)

Questions 17-28 now comprise all of the above interval possibilities (i.e. harmonic minor 2nd and major 7th intervals). For each question, write the notes on the staff, together with the solfeg and interval description.

17.   18.   19.   20.

Key of F

Solfeg: ___ ___   ___ ___   ___ ___   ___ ___
Interval Description: _____   _____   _____   _____

21.   22.   23.   24.

Key of D

Solfeg: ___ ___   ___ ___   ___ ___   ___ ___
Interval Description: _____   _____   _____   _____

25.   26.   27.   28.

Key of Bb

Solfeg: ___ ___   ___ ___   ___ ___   ___ ___
Interval Description: _____   _____   _____   _____

(Questions 29-36 now include all intervals studied prior to this chapter, within the range of possibilities).

29.   30.   31.   32.

Key of F

Solfeg: ___ ___   ___ ___   ___ ___   ___ ___
Interval Description: _____   _____   _____   _____

(5.2. contd)

33.   34.   35.   36.

Key of D

Solfeg: _____ _____   _____ _____   _____ _____ _____   _____ _____

Interval Description: _____   _____   _____   _____

5.3.   MELODIC DICTATION/TRANSCRIPTION

These 10 questions consist of melodies based on this chapter's material. _Listen for the new minor 2nd and major 7th intervals being used._ Write your answers below:-

1.

2.

3.

4.

5.

6.

7.

8.

9.

10.

5.4. *Diatonic Triad Identification*

These questions consist of an individual root-position diatonic triad which will either be the **I**, **II**, **III**, **IV**, **V** or **VI** of the respective key. Please write the chord symbol, followed by the (roman numeral) chord function in parentheses.

Questions 1-6 are in the key of D.
Options are:- **D (I)**, **Emi (II)**, **F#mi (III)**, **G (IV)**, **A (V)**, or **Bmi (VI)**.

1.	_____ ( )		4.	_____ ( )
2.	_____ ( )		5.	_____ ( )
3.	_____ ( )		6.	_____ ( )

Questions 7-12 are in the key of Bb.
Options are:- **Bb (I)**, **Cmi (II)**, **Dmi (III)**, **Eb (IV)**, **F (V)**, or **Gmi (VI)**.

7.	_____ ( )		10.	_____ ( )
8.	_____ ( )		11	_____ ( )
9.	_____ ( )		12.	_____ ( )

Questions 13-22 consist of melodies to which diatonic triads and bass notes are to be added. Within each key the harmonization options are either the **I**, **II**, **III**, **IV**, **V** or **VI** diatonic triads.

Key of C   13.   14.

Key of G   15.   16.

(5.4. contd)

Key of F   17.   18.

Key of D   19.   20.

Key of Bb   21.   22.

Questions 23-34 consist of diatonic triad 'pairs' again using combinations of the **I**, **II**, **III**, **IV**, **V** or **VI** diatonic triads of the key. Write your answers (chord symbols) below:-

Key of D

23. _____ _____   26. _____ _____
24 _____ _____   27. _____ _____
25. _____ _____   28. _____ _____

Key of Bb

29. _____ _____   32. _____ _____
30. _____ _____   33. _____ _____
31. _____ _____   34. _____ _____

(5.4. contd)

Questions 35-46 consist of progressions containing 3 triads each, again using combinations of the **I**, **II**, **III**, **IV**, **V** or **VI** of the key. Write your answers (chord symbols) below:-

Key of D

35. _____ _____ _____   38. _____ _____ _____
36 _____ _____ _____   39. _____ _____ _____
37. _____ _____ _____   40. _____ _____ _____

Key of Bb

41. _____ _____ _____   44. _____ _____ _____
42. _____ _____ _____   45. _____ _____ _____
43. _____ _____ _____   46. _____ _____ _____

5.5.   **BASS LINE DICTATION/TRANSCRIPTION**

Write our your answers below:-

1.   2.

3.   4.

5.   6.

7.   8.

9.   10.

6. **_Eartraining Assignments - Workbook Answers_**

_6.1._ **_Melodic Interval Identification answers_**

(Minor 2nds)

1.	MI	-	FA		7.	FA	-	MI
2.	DO	-	TI		8.	DO	-	TI
3.	TI	-	DO		9.	MI	-	FA
4.	FA	-	MI		10.	TI	-	DO
5.	TI	-	DO		11.	TI	-	DO
6.	MI	-	FA		12.	FA	-	MI

(Major 7ths)

13.	TI	-	DO		19.	DO	-	TI
14.	FA	-	MI		20.	MI	-	FA
15.	DO	-	TI		21.	FA	-	MI
16.	MI	-	FA		22.	TI	-	DO
17.	TI	-	DO		23.	DO	-	TI
18.	DO	-	TI		24.	MI	-	FA

Key of G

Solfeg: **MI FA** **DO TI** **MI FA** **DO TI**
Interval Description: **Mi2** **Ma7** **Ma7** **Mi2**

(6.1. contd)

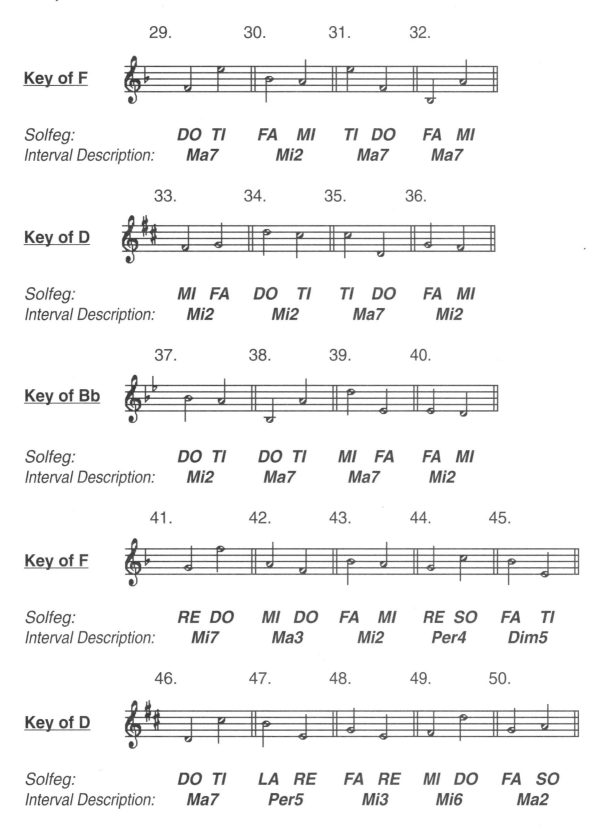

Key of F

29.   30.   31.   32.

Solfeg: **DO TI FA MI TI DO FA MI**
Interval Description: **Ma7   Mi2   Ma7   Ma7**

Key of D

33.   34.   35.   36.

Solfeg: **MI FA DO TI TI DO FA MI**
Interval Description: **Mi2   Mi2   Ma7   Mi2**

Key of Bb

37.   38.   39.   40.

Solfeg: **DO TI DO TI MI FA FA MI**
Interval Description: **Mi2   Ma7   Ma7   Mi2**

Key of F

41.   42.   43.   44.   45.

Solfeg: **RE DO MI DO FA MI RE SO FA TI**
Interval Description: **Mi7   Ma3   Mi2   Per4   Dim5**

Key of D

46.   47.   48.   49.   50.

Solfeg: **DO TI LA RE FA RE MI DO FA SO**
Interval Description: **Ma7   Per5   Mi3   Mi6   Ma2**

6.2. Harmonic Interval Identification answers

(Minor 2nds)

1.	MI	-	FA	5.	TI	-	DO
2.	TI	-	DO	6.	MI	-	FA
3.	MI	-	FA	7.	MI	-	FA
4.	TI	-	DO	8.	TI	-	DO

(Major 7ths)

9.	DO	-	TI	13.	FA	-	MI
10.	FA	-	MI	14.	DO	-	TI
11.	FA	-	MI	15.	DO	-	TI
12.	DO	-	TI	16.	FA	-	MI

(6.2. contd)

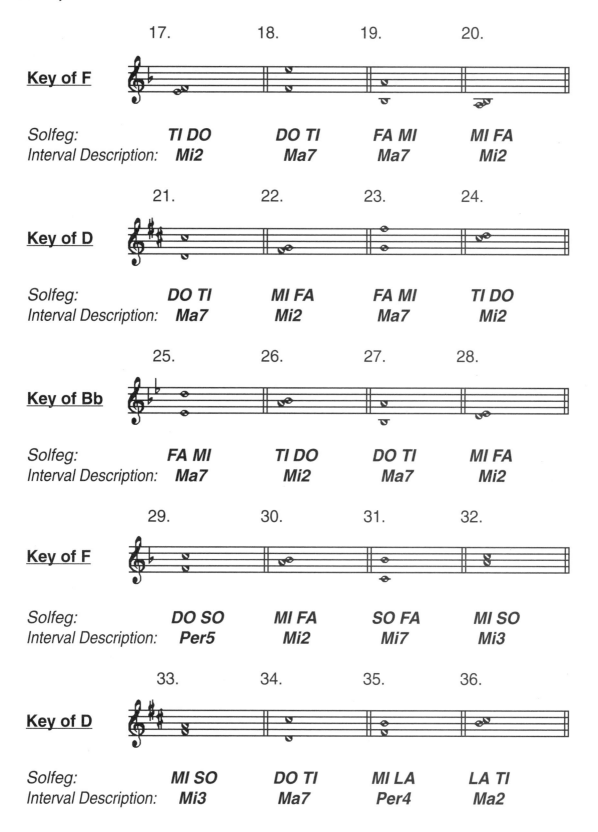

	17.	18.	19.	20.
Solfeg:	**TI DO**	**DO TI**	**FA MI**	**MI FA**
Interval Description:	**Mi2**	**Ma7**	**Ma7**	**Mi2**

	21.	22.	23.	24.
Solfeg:	**DO TI**	**MI FA**	**FA MI**	**TI DO**
Interval Description:	**Ma7**	**Mi2**	**Ma7**	**Mi2**

	25.	26.	27.	28.
Solfeg:	**FA MI**	**TI DO**	**DO TI**	**MI FA**
Interval Description:	**Ma7**	**Mi2**	**Ma7**	**Mi2**

	29.	30.	31.	32.
Solfeg:	**DO SO**	**MI FA**	**SO FA**	**MI SO**
Interval Description:	**Per5**	**Mi2**	**Mi7**	**Mi3**

	33.	34.	35.	36.
Solfeg:	**MI SO**	**DO TI**	**MI LA**	**LA TI**
Interval Description:	**Mi3**	**Ma7**	**Per4**	**Ma2**

169

6.3.   **MELODIC DICTATION/TRANSCRIPTION ANSWERS**

6.4. Diatonic Triad Identification answers

(individual triad recognition)

Key of D

1.	**G**	(IV)		4.	**A**	(V)
2.	**Emi**	(II)		5.	**F#mi**	(III)
3.	**Bmi**	(VI)		6.	**D**	(I)

Key of Bb

7.	**Gmi**	(VI)		10.	**Eb**	(IV)
8.	**Bb**	(I)		11.	**F**	(V)
9.	**Dmi**	(III)		12.	**Cmi**	(II)

(harmonization questions)

Key of C

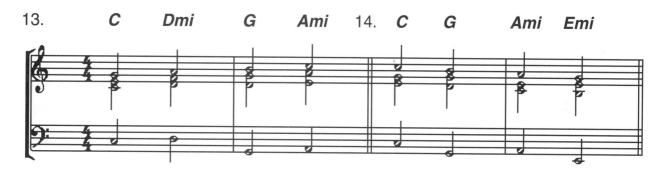

Key of G

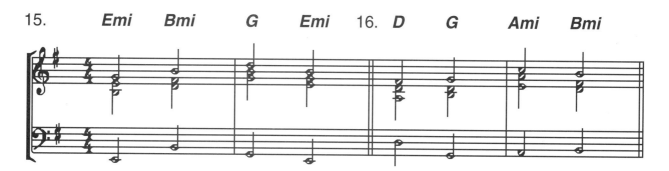

(6.4. contd)

Key of F

Key of D

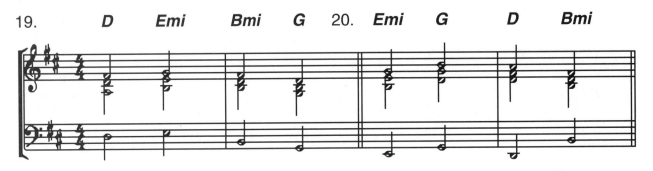

Key of Bb

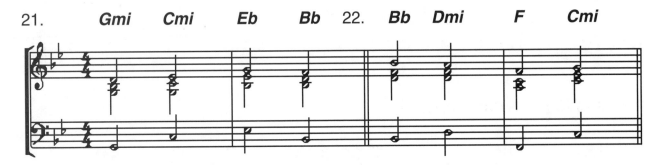

(6.4. contd)

(2-chord progressions)

Key of D

23.	G	D
24.	Emi	A
25.	D	Emi

26.	Bmi	G
27.	D	A
28.	D	Bmi

Key of Bb

29.	Bb	F
30.	Cmi	Eb
31.	Gmi	Cmi

32.	Eb	Bb
33.	Eb	F
34.	Bb	Cmi

(3-chord progressions)

Key of D

35.	D	Emi	F#mi
36.	D	A	Bmi
37.	G	A	Bmi

38.	F#mi	D	Emi
39.	G	A	F#mi
40.	D	Emi	G

Key of Bb

41.	Bb	Dmi	Cmi
42.	Bb	F	Gmi
43.	Eb	Bb	F

44.	Gmi	Eb	Bb
45.	F	Bb	Cmi
46.	Bb	F	Eb

CHAPTER SEVEN

6.5.   **BASS LINE DICTATION/TRANSCRIPTION ANSWERS**

1.

2.

3.

4.

5.

6.

7.

8.

9.

10.

Review and further drill on all subject areas

1. Theory and Notation

1.1. This final chapter will primarily be used for review and drill purposes. Please refer to previous drills and exercises in the text as required.

1.2. This chapter will also introduce some further rhythmic combinations based upon anticipating beat **3** by an eighth note (see Chapter 7 text paragraph **1.7.**), as follows:-

a)  *Dotted quarter-eighth tied to a quarter-quarter*

b)  *Dotted quarter-eighth tied to a quarter-eighth-eighth*

c)  *Dotted quarter-eighth tied to an eighth-eighth-quarter*

d)  *Dotted quarter-eighth tied to an eighth-eighth-eighth-eighth*

1.3.   In a melodic context these rhythmic patterns might occur as follows:-

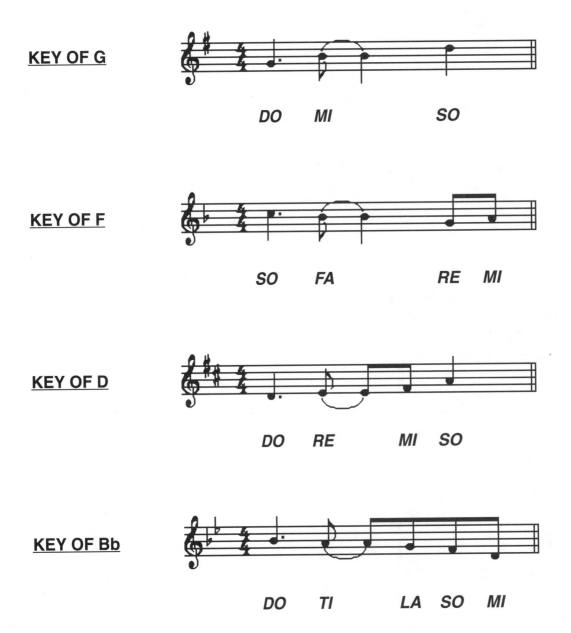

KEY OF G

DO   MI   SO

KEY OF F

SO   FA   RE   MI

KEY OF D

DO   RE   MI   SO

KEY OF Bb

DO   TI   LA   SO   MI

2. _Class/Study Activities_

2.1. _Interval singing and recognition_

- Recognition of (melodic and harmonic) all interval types covered so far, in all keys studied.

2.2. _Melodic dictation/transcription_

- Transcribing melodies containing all intervals and rhythmic combinations covered so far, in all keys studied.

2.3. _Diatonic triad recognition_

- Recognition of **I**, **II**, **III**, **IV**, **V** and **VI** diatonic triads in root position, in all keys studied.
- Harmonization of (given) 4-note melodies with **I**, **II**, **III**, **IV**, **V** and **VI** diatonic triads, in all keys studied.
- Identifying 2- and 3-chord progressions using the **I**, **II**, **III**, **IV**, **V** and **VI** diatonic triads, in all keys studied.

2.4. _Bass line dictation/transcription_

- Transcribing bass lines containing all intervals and rhythmic combinations covered so far, in all keys studied.

(2.2.)   __MELODIES FOR SINGING AND TRANSCRIPTION__

3. _Theory Assignments_

3.1. _Supplementary Worksheets - Keys of C, G, F, D and Bb._

- Review as required, and ensure that all intervals and diatonic triads are complete for the above keys - refer to previous text as necessary.

4. _Eartraining Tapes Available (see page iv) - tape contents for this chapter_

4.1. _The Eartraining tape available for Chapter 8 consists of the following:-_

- melodic interval identification questions (all diatonic intervals) ascending and descending
    - you may fill out your answers in section **5.1.**
    - you may check against correct answers in section **6.1.**

- harmonic interval identification questions (all diatonic intervals)
    - you may fill out your answers in section **5.2.**
    - you may check against correct answers in section **6.2.**

- melodic dictation/transcription questions
    - you may fill out your answers in section **5.3.**
    - you may check against correct answers in section **6.3.**

- diatonic triad recognition
    - you may fill out your answers in section **5.4.**
    - you may check against correct answers in section **6.4.**

- bass line dictation/transcription
    - you may fill out your answers in section **5.5.**
    - you may check against correct answers in section **6.5.**

5. **_Eartraining Assignments - Workbook Questions_**

(fill out your answers here)

_5.1._ **_Melodic Interval Identification_**

Questions 1-16 consist of melodic intervals (ascending or descending). The options now include all melodic intervals previously covered. For each question, write the notes on the staff, together with the solfeg and interval description.

1.   2.   3.   4.

Key of G

Solfeg: ____ ____ ____ ____ ____ ____ ____ ____
Interval Description: ____ ____ ____ ____

5.   6.   7.   8.

Key of F

Solfeg: ____ ____ ____ ____ ____ ____ ____ ____
Interval Description: ____ ____ ____ ____

9.   10.   11.   12.

Key of D

Soifeg: ____ ____ ____ ____ ____ ____ ____ ____
Interval Description: ____ ____ ____ ____

13.   14.   15.   16.

Key of Bb

Solfeg: ____ ____ ____ ____ ____ ____ ____ ____
Interval Description: ____ ____ ____ ____

5.2. Harmonic Interval Identification

Questions 1-16 consist of intervals played harmonically i.e. both tones played simultaneously. The options now include all harmonic intervals previously covered. For each question, write the notes on the staff, together with the solfeg and interval description.

1.   2.   3.   4.

Key of G

Solfeg:
Interval Description:

5.   6.   7.   8.

Key of F

Solfeg:
Interval Description:

9.   10.   11.   12.

Key of D

Soifeg:
Interval Description:

13.   14.   15.   16.

Key of Bb

Solfeg:
Interval Description:

5.3.   **MELODIC DICTATION/TRANSCRIPTION**

· These 5 questions consist of melodies using all intervals and rhythms studied so far. Write your answers below:

1.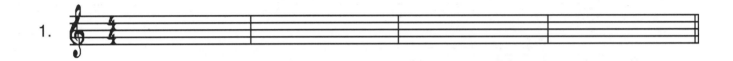

2.

3.

4.

5.

5.4. Diatonic Triad Identification

Questions 1-10 consist of melodies to which diatonic triads and bass notes are to be added. Within each key all diatonic triads studied so far (i.e. all except the **VII**) are available as harmonization options.

Key of C   1.   2.

Key of G   3.   4.

Key of F   5.   6.

Key of D   7.   8.

(5.4. contd)

Key of Bb   9.   10.

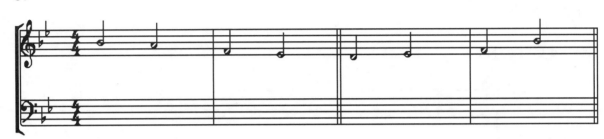

Questions 11-22 consist of diatonic triad 'pairs' again using combinations of the **I**, **II**, **III**, **IV**, **V** or **VI** diatonic triads of the key. Write your answers (chord symbols) below:-

Key of F

11. _____ _____   14. _____ _____
12 _____ _____   15. _____ _____
13. _____ _____   16. _____ _____

Key of D

17. _____ _____   20. _____ _____
18. _____ _____   21. _____ _____
19. _____ _____   22. _____ _____

Questions 23-34 consist of progressions containing 3 triads each, again using combinations of the **I**, **II**, **III**, **IV**, **V** or **VI** diatonic triads of the key. Write your answers (chord symbols) below:-

Key of C

23. _____ _____ _____   26. _____ _____ _____
24 _____ _____ _____   27. _____ _____ _____
25. _____ _____ _____   28. _____ _____ _____

Key of G

29. _____ _____ _____   32. _____ _____ _____
30. _____ _____ _____   33. _____ _____ _____
31. _____ _____ _____   34. _____ _____ _____

5.5.   **BASS LINE DICTATION/TRANSCRIPTION**

Write our your answers below:-

1.   2.

3.   4.

5.   6.

7.   8.

9.   10.

CHAPTER EIGHT

6. Eartraining Assignments - Workbook Answers

6.1. Melodic Interval Identification answers

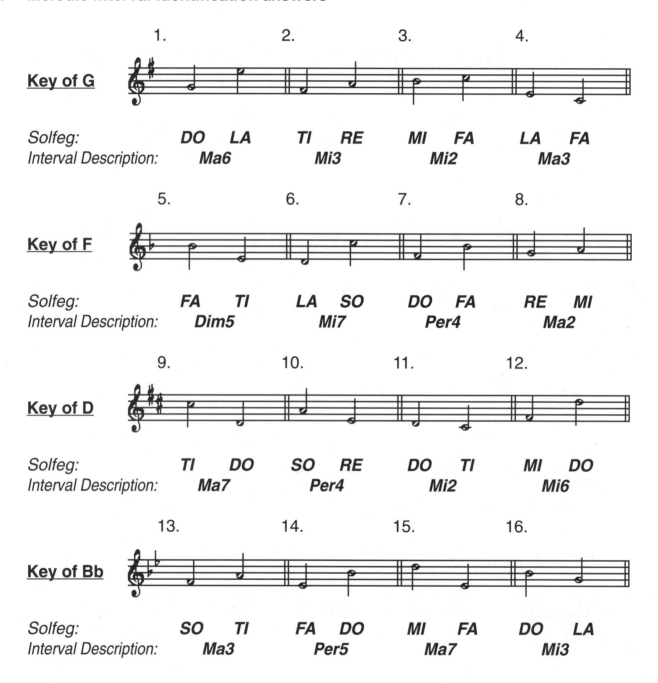

Key of G

	1.	2.	3.	4.
Solfeg:	DO LA	TI RE	MI FA	LA FA
Interval Description:	Ma6	Mi3	Mi2	Ma3

Key of F

	5.	6.	7.	8.
Solfeg:	FA TI	LA SO	DO FA	RE MI
Interval Description:	Dim5	Mi7	Per4	Ma2

Key of D

	9.	10.	11.	12.
Solfeg:	TI DO	SO RE	DO TI	MI DO
Interval Description:	Ma7	Per4	Mi2	Mi6

Key of Bb

	13.	14.	15.	16.
Solfeg:	SO TI	FA DO	MI FA	DO LA
Interval Description:	Ma3	Per5	Ma7	Mi3

6.2. *Harmonic Interval Identification answers*

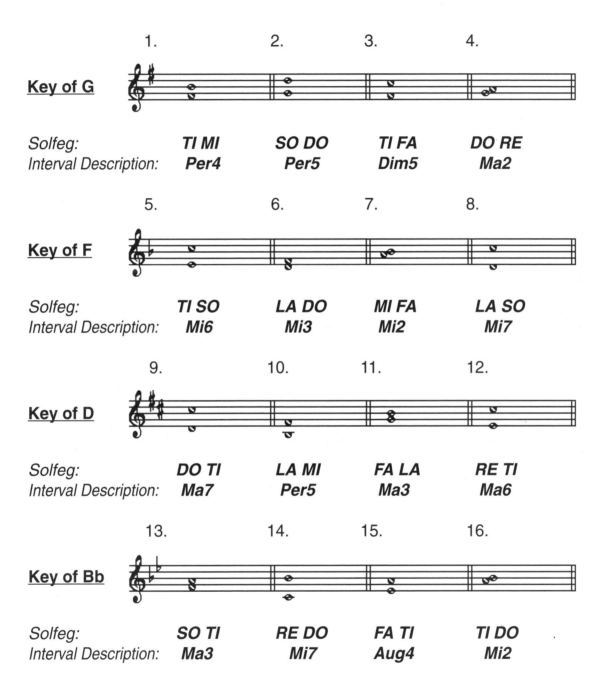

Key of G

	1.	2.	3.	4.
Solfeg:	**TI MI**	**SO DO**	**TI FA**	**DO RE**
Interval Description:	**Per4**	**Per5**	**Dim5**	**Ma2**

Key of F

	5.	6.	7.	8.
Solfeg:	**TI SO**	**LA DO**	**MI FA**	**LA SO**
Interval Description:	**Mi6**	**Mi3**	**Mi2**	**Mi7**

Key of D

	9.	10.	11.	12.
Solfeg:	**DO TI**	**LA MI**	**FA LA**	**RE TI**
Interval Description:	**Ma7**	**Per5**	**Ma3**	**Ma6**

Key of Bb

	13.	14.	15.	16.
Solfeg:	**SO TI**	**RE DO**	**FA TI**	**TI DO**
Interval Description:	**Ma3**	**Mi7**	**Aug4**	**Mi2**

6.3. **MELODIC DICTATION/TRANSCRIPTION ANSWERS**

6.4. Diatonic Triad Identification answers

(harmonization questions)

Key of C

Key of G

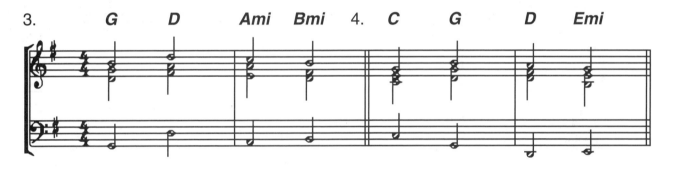

Key of F

(6.4. contd)

Key of D

7.   *D*   *Emi*   *F#mi*   *Bmi*   8.   *G*   *D*   *A*   *F#mi*

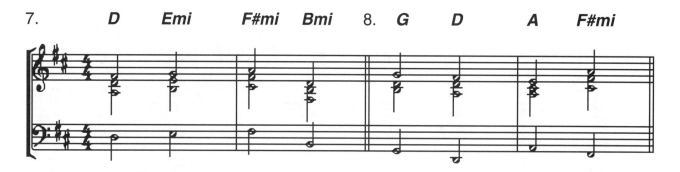

Key of Bb

9.   *Gmi*   *F*   *Bb*   *Cmi*   10. *Dmi*   *Eb*   *Bb*   *Cmi*

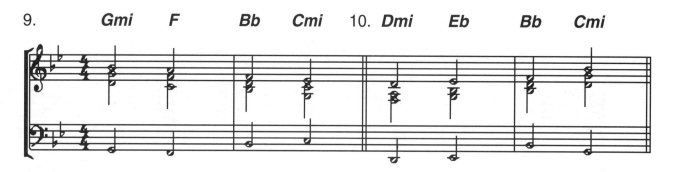

(2-chord progressions)

Key of F

11.   *F*   *C*   14.   *F*   *Bb*

12.   *Bb*   *Dmi*   15.   *C*   *Dmi*

13.   *Ami*   *Gmi*   16.   *Ami*   *F*

Key of D

17.   *D*   *A*   20.   *Emi*   *G*

18.   *G*   *D*   21.   *Bmi*   *D*

19.   *G*   *F#mi*   22.   *Bmi*   *G*

(6.4. contd)

(3-chord progressions)

Key of C

23.	*C*	*F*	*C*		26.	*Emi*	*Dmi*	*C*
24.	*C*	*Ami*	*F*		27.	*Dmi*	*F*	*C*
25.	*F*	*C*	*Ami*		28.	*F*	*G*	*Emi*

Key of G

29.	*Bmi*	*D*	*Emi*		32.	*Ami*	*C*	*G*
30.	*C*	*D*	*C*		33.	*G*	*Bmi*	*Emi*
31.	*C*	*Emi*	*D*		34.	*D*	*Emi*	*C*

6.5.　　　　　　**BASS LINE DICTATION/TRANSCRIPTION ANSWERS**

Supplementary Worksheets - Key of C

RESOLUTIONS

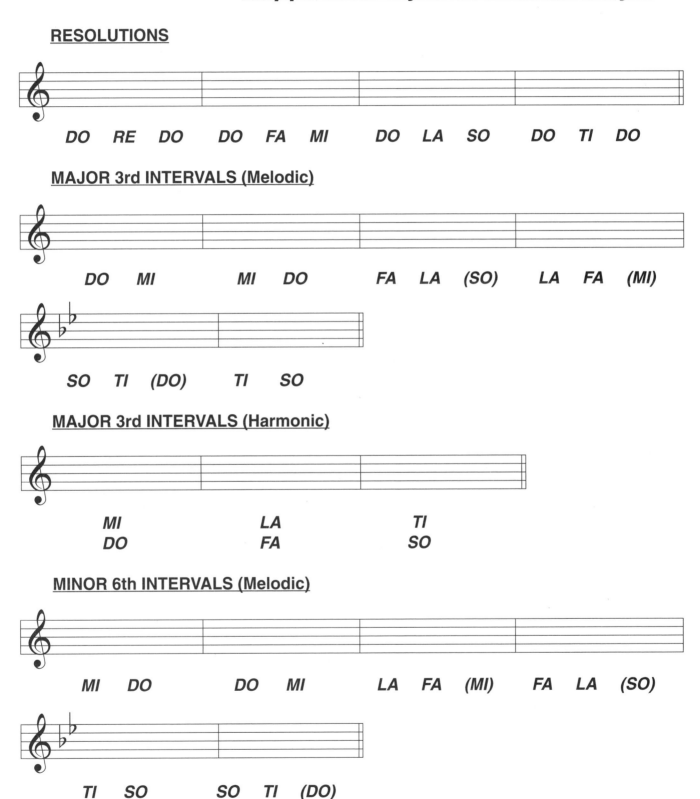

DO   RE   DO   DO   FA   MI   DO   LA   SO   DO   TI   DO

MAJOR 3rd INTERVALS (Melodic)

DO   MI   MI   DO   FA   LA   (SO)   LA   FA   (MI)

SO   TI   (DO)   TI   SO

MAJOR 3rd INTERVALS (Harmonic)

MI   LA   TI
DO   FA   SO

MINOR 6th INTERVALS (Melodic)

MI   DO   DO   MI   LA   FA   (MI)   FA   LA   (SO)

TI   SO   SO   TI   (DO)

193

(Key of C contd)

MINOR 6th INTERVALS (Harmonic)

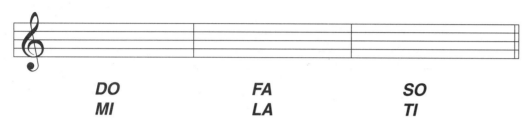

DO	FA	SO
MI	LA	TI

MINOR 3rd INTERVALS (Melodic)

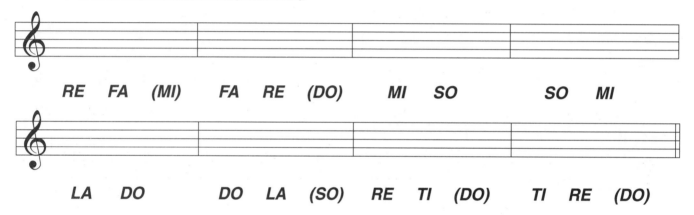

RE FA (MI)   FA RE (DO)   MI SO   SO MI

LA DO   DO LA (SO)   RE TI (DO)   TI RE (DO)

MINOR 3rd INTERVALS (Harmonic)

FA	SO	DO	RE
RE	MI	LA	TI

MAJOR 6th INTERVALS (Melodic)

DO LA (SO)   LA DO   RE TI (DO)   TI RE (DO)

FA RE (DO)   RE FA (MI)   SO MI   MI SO

(Key of C contd)

MAJOR 6th INTERVALS (Harmonic)

LA   TI   RE   MI
DO   RE   FA   SO

PERFECT 4th INTERVALS (Melodic)

DO FA (MI) FA DO   RE SO   SO RE (DO)

MI LA (SO) LA MI   SO DO   DO SO

LA RE (DO) RE LA (SO)   TI MI   MI TI (DO)

PERFECT 4th INTERVALS (Harmonic)

FA   SO   LA   DO   RE   MI
DO   RE   MI   SO   LA   TI

(Key of C contd)

PERFECT 5th INTERVALS (Melodic)

DO   SO   SO   DO   RE   LA   (SO)   LA   RE   (DO)

MI   TI   (DO)   TI   MI   FA   DO   DO   FA   (MI)

SO   RE   (DO)   RE   SO   LA   MI   MI   LA   (SO)

PERFECT 5th INTERVALS (Harmonic)

SO   LA   TI   DO   RE   MI
DO   RE   MI   FA   SO   LA

AUGMENTED 4TH/DIMINISHED 5th INTERVALS (Melodic)

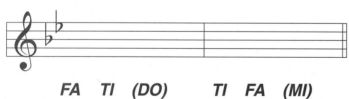

FA   TI   (DO)   TI   FA   (MI)

AUGMENTED 4TH/DIMINISHED 5th INTERVALS (Harmonic)

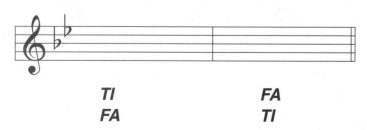

TI   FA
FA   TI

(Key of C contd)

MAJOR 2nd INTERVALS (Melodic)

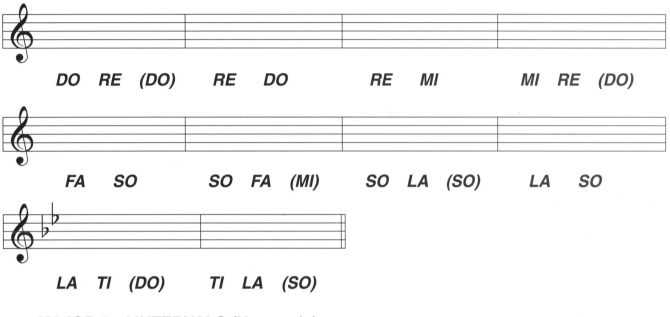

DO RE (DO)   RE DO   RE MI   MI RE (DO)

FA SO   SO FA (MI)   SO LA (SO)   LA SO

LA TI (DO)   TI LA (SO)

MAJOR 2nd INTERVALS (Harmonic)

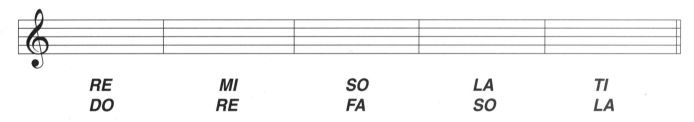

RE	MI	SO	LA	TI
DO	RE	FA	SO	LA

MINOR 7th INTERVALS (Melodic)

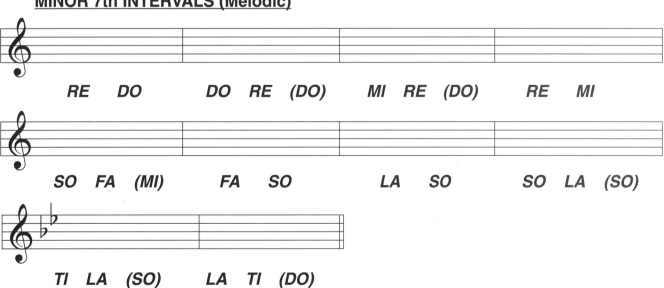

RE DO   DO RE (DO)   MI RE (DO)   RE MI

SO FA (MI)   FA SO   LA SO   SO LA (SO)

TI LA (SO)   LA TI (DO)

(Key of C contd)

MINOR 7th INTERVALS (Harmonic)

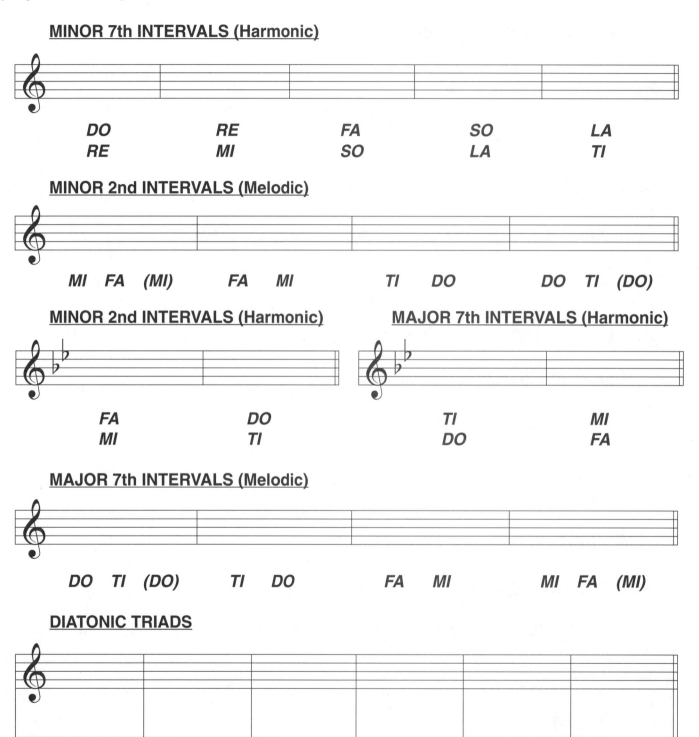

DO	RE	FA	SO	LA
RE	MI	SO	LA	TI

MINOR 2nd INTERVALS (Melodic)

MI FA (MI)   FA MI   TI DO   DO TI (DO)

MINOR 2nd INTERVALS (Harmonic)   MAJOR 7th INTERVALS (Harmonic)

FA	DO	TI	MI
MI	TI	DO	FA

MAJOR 7th INTERVALS (Melodic)

DO TI (DO)   TI DO   FA MI   MI FA (MI)

DIATONIC TRIADS

I   II   III   IV   V   VI

Supplementary Worksheets - Key of G

RESOLUTIONS

DO RE DO   DO FA MI   DO LA SO   DO TI DO

MAJOR 3rd INTERVALS (Melodic)

DO MI   MI DO   FA LA (SO) LA FA (MI)

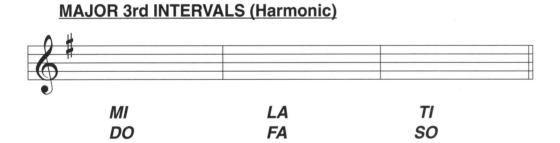

SO TI (DO)   TI SO

MAJOR 3rd INTERVALS (Harmonic)

MI   LA   TI
DO   FA   SO

MINOR 6th INTERVALS (Melodic)

MI DO   DO MI   LA FA (MI) FA LA (SO)

TI SO   SO TI (DO)

(Key of G contd)

MINOR 6th INTERVALS (Harmonic)

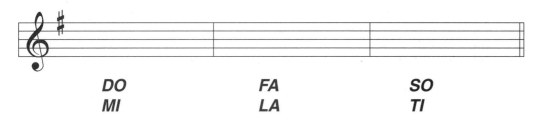

DO	FA	SO
MI	LA	TI

MINOR 3rd INTERVALS (Melodic)

RE FA (MI)	FA RE (DO)	MI SO	SO MI
LA DO	DO LA (SO)	RE TI (DO)	TI RE (DO)

MINOR 3rd INTERVALS (Harmonic)

FA	SO	DO	RE
RE	MI	LA	TI

MAJOR 6th INTERVALS (Melodic)

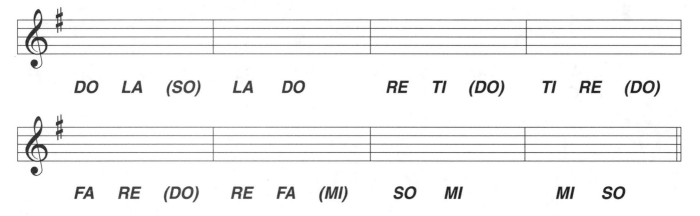

DO LA (SO)	LA DO	RE TI (DO)	TI RE (DO)
FA RE (DO)	RE FA (MI)	SO MI	MI SO

(Key of G contd)

MAJOR 6th INTERVALS (Harmonic)

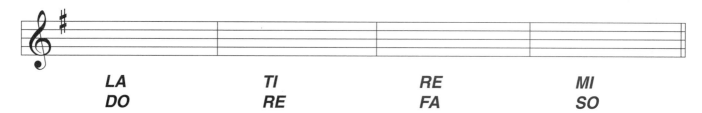

LA	TI	RE	MI
DO	RE	FA	SO

PERFECT 4th INTERVALS (Melodic)

DO FA (MI) FA DO   RE SO   SO RE (DO)

MI LA (SO) LA MI   SO DO   DO SO

LA RE (DO) RE LA (SO)   TI MI   MI TI (DO)

PERFECT 4th INTERVALS (Harmonic)

FA	SO	LA	DO	RE	MI
DO	RE	MI	SO	LA	TI

(Key of G contd)

PERFECT 5th INTERVALS (Melodic)

DO SO   SO DO   RE LA (SO)   LA RE (DO)

MI TI (DO)   TI MI   FA DO   DO FA (MI)

SO RE (DO)   RE SO   LA MI   MI LA (SO)

PERFECT 5th INTERVALS (Harmonic)

SO   LA   TI   DO   RE   MI
DO   RE   MI   FA   SO   LA

AUGMENTED 4TH/DIMINISHED 5th INTERVALS (Melodic)

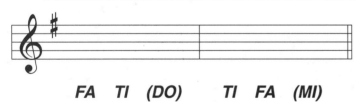

FA TI (DO)   TI FA (MI)

AUGMENTED 4TH/DIMINISHED 5th INTERVALS (Harmonic)

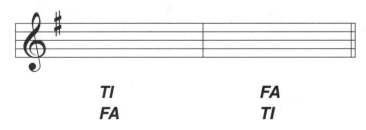

TI   FA
FA   TI

(Key of G contd)

MAJOR 2nd INTERVALS (Melodic)

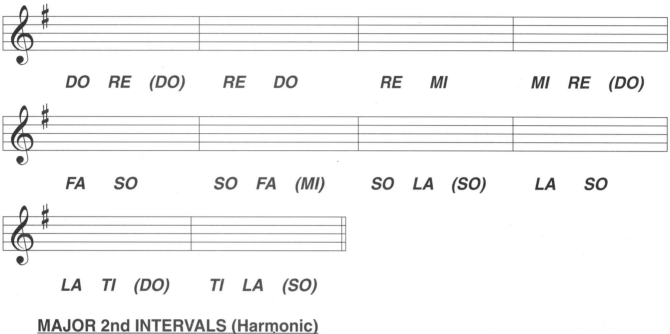

DO RE (DO)   RE DO   RE MI   MI RE (DO)

FA SO   SO FA (MI)   SO LA (SO)   LA SO

LA TI (DO)   TI LA (SO)

MAJOR 2nd INTERVALS (Harmonic)

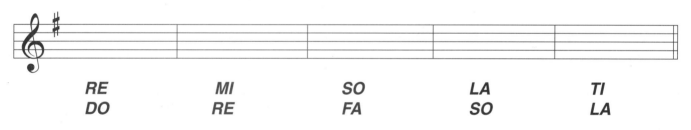

RE   MI   SO   LA   TI
DO   RE   FA   SO   LA

MINOR 7th INTERVALS (Melodic)

RE DO   DO RE (DO)   MI RE (DO)   RE MI

SO FA (MI)   FA SO   LA SO   SO LA (SO)

TI LA (SO)   LA TI (DO)

(Key of G contd)

MINOR 7th INTERVALS (Harmonic)

| DO | RE | FA | SO | LA |
| RE | MI | SO | LA | TI |

MINOR 2nd INTERVALS (Melodic)

MI FA (MI)   FA MI   TI DO   DO TI (DO)

MINOR 2nd INTERVALS (Harmonic)   MAJOR 7th INTERVALS (Harmonic)

| FA | DO | | TI | MI |
| MI | TI | | DO | FA |

MAJOR 7th INTERVALS (Melodic)

DO TI (DO)   TI DO   FA MI   MI FA (MI)

DIATONIC TRIADS

I   II   III   IV   V   VI

Supplementary Worksheets - Key of F

RESOLUTIONS

DO   RE   DO   DO   FA   MI   DO   LA   SO   DO   TI   DO

MAJOR 3rd INTERVALS (Melodic)

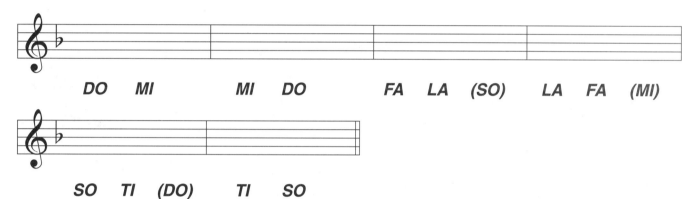

DO   MI   MI   DO   FA   LA   (SO)   LA   FA   (MI)

SO   TI   (DO)   TI   SO

MAJOR 3rd INTERVALS (Harmonic)

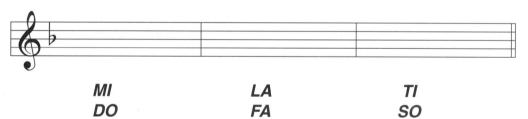

MI   LA   TI
DO   FA   SO

MINOR 6th INTERVALS (Melodic)

MI   DO   DO   MI   LA   FA   (MI)   FA   LA   (SO)

TI   SO   SO   TI   (DO)

SUPPLEMENTARY WORKSHEETS

(Key of F contd)

MINOR 6th INTERVALS (Harmonic)

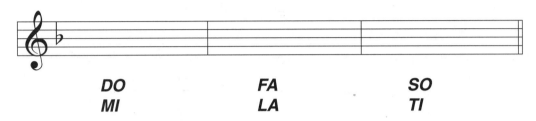

DO	FA	SO
MI	LA	TI

MINOR 3rd INTERVALS (Melodic)

RE FA (MI)   FA RE (DO)   MI SO   SO MI

LA DO   DO LA (SO)   RE TI (DO)   TI RE (DO)

MINOR 3rd INTERVALS (Harmonic)

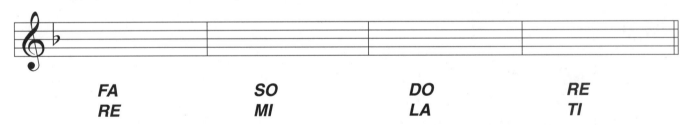

FA	SO	DO	RE
RE	MI	LA	TI

MAJOR 6th INTERVALS (Melodic)

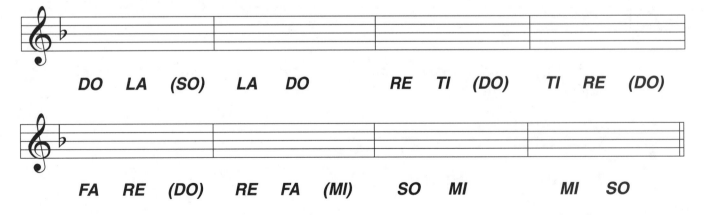

DO LA (SO)   LA DO   RE TI (DO)   TI RE (DO)

FA RE (DO)   RE FA (MI)   SO MI   MI SO

(Key of F contd)

MAJOR 6th INTERVALS (Harmonic)

LA	TI	RE	MI
DO	RE	FA	SO

PERFECT 4th INTERVALS (Melodic)

DO FA (MI)   FA DO   RE SO   SO RE (DO)

MI LA (SO)   LA MI   SO DO   DO SO

LA RE (DO)   RE LA (SO)   TI MI   MI TI (DO)

PERFECT 4th INTERVALS (Harmonic)

FA	SO	LA	DO	RE	MI
DO	RE	MI	SO	LA	TI

SUPPLEMENTARY WORKSHEETS

(Key of F contd)

PERFECT 5th INTERVALS (Melodic)

DO   SO   SO   DO   RE   LA (SO)   LA   RE (DO)

MI   TI (DO)   TI   MI   FA   DO   DO   FA (MI)

SO   RE (DO)   RE   SO   LA   MI   MI   LA (SO)

PERFECT 5th INTERVALS (Harmonic)

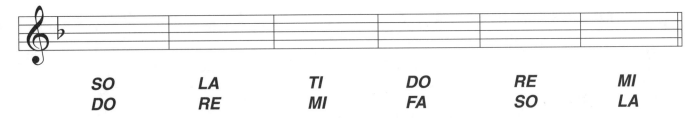

SO   LA   TI   DO   RE   MI
DO   RE   MI   FA   SO   LA

AUGMENTED 4TH/DIMINISHED 5th INTERVALS (Melodic)

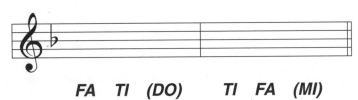

FA   TI (DO)   TI   FA (MI)

AUGMENTED 4TH/DIMINISHED 5th INTERVALS (Harmonic)

TI   FA
FA   TI

(Key of F contd)

MAJOR 2nd INTERVALS (Melodic)

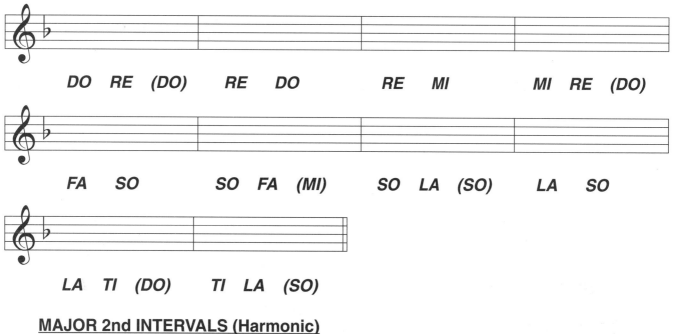

DO RE (DO)   RE DO   RE MI   MI RE (DO)

FA SO   SO FA (MI)   SO LA (SO)   LA SO

LA TI (DO)   TI LA (SO)

MAJOR 2nd INTERVALS (Harmonic)

RE   MI   SO   LA   TI
DO   RE   FA   SO   LA

MINOR 7th INTERVALS (Melodic)

RE DO   DO RE (DO)   MI RE (DO)   RE MI

SO FA (MI)   FA SO   LA SO   SO LA (SO)

TI LA (SO)   LA TI (DO)

(Key of F contd)

MINOR 7th INTERVALS (Harmonic)

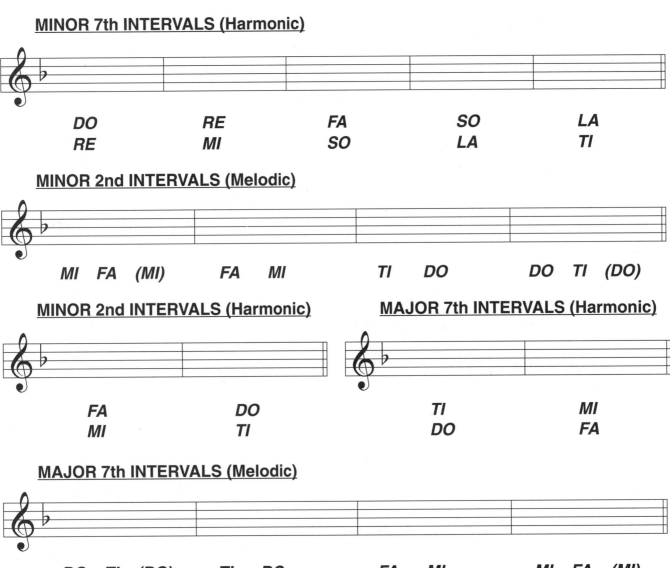

| DO | RE | FA | SO | LA |
| RE | MI | SO | LA | TI |

MINOR 2nd INTERVALS (Melodic)

MI FA (MI)   FA MI   TI DO   DO TI (DO)

MINOR 2nd INTERVALS (Harmonic)   MAJOR 7th INTERVALS (Harmonic)

| FA | DO | | TI | MI |
| MI | TI | | DO | FA |

MAJOR 7th INTERVALS (Melodic)

DO TI (DO)   TI DO   FA MI   MI FA (MI)

DIATONIC TRIADS

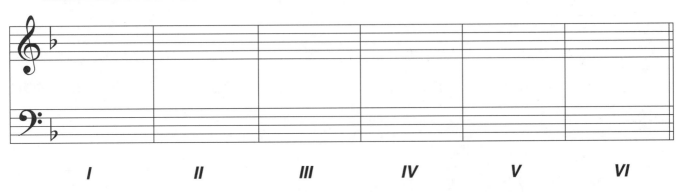

I   II   III   IV   V   VI

Supplementary Worksheets - Key of D

RESOLUTIONS

DO RE DO   DO FA MI   DO LA SO   DO TI DO

MAJOR 3rd INTERVALS (Melodic)

DO MI   MI DO   FA LA (SO)   LA FA (MI)

SO TI (DO)   TI SO

MAJOR 3rd INTERVALS (Harmonic)

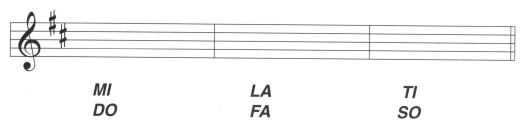

MI   LA   TI
DO   FA   SO

MINOR 6th INTERVALS (Melodic)

MI DO   DO MI   LA FA (MI)   FA LA (SO)

TI SO   SO TI (DO)

(Key of D contd)

MINOR 6th INTERVALS (Harmonic)

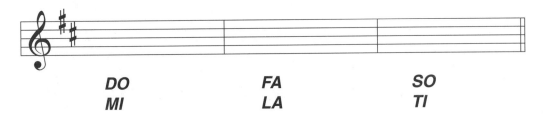

DO   FA   SO
MI   LA   TI

MINOR 3rd INTERVALS (Melodic)

RE   FA   (MI)   FA   RE   (DO)   MI   SO   SO   MI

LA   DO   DO   LA   (SO)   RE   TI   (DO)   TI   RE   (DO)

MINOR 3rd INTERVALS (Harmonic)

FA   SO   DO   RE
RE   MI   LA   TI

MAJOR 6th INTERVALS (Melodic)

DO   LA   (SO)   LA   DO   RE   TI   (DO)   TI   RE   (DO)

FA   RE   (DO)   RE   FA   (MI)   SO   MI   MI   SO

(Key of D contd)

MAJOR 6th INTERVALS (Harmonic)

LA	TI	RE	MI
DO	RE	FA	SO

PERFECT 4th INTERVALS (Melodic)

DO FA (MI)   FA DO   RE SO   SO RE (DO)

MI LA (SO)   LA MI   SO DO   DO SO

LA RE (DO)   RE LA (SO)   TI MI   MI TI (DO)

PERFECT 4th INTERVALS (Harmonic)

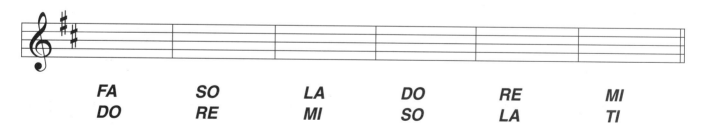

FA	SO	LA	DO	RE	MI
DO	RE	MI	SO	LA	TI

(Key of D contd)

PERFECT 5th INTERVALS (Melodic)

DO SO   SO DO   RE LA (SO)   LA RE (DO)

MI TI (DO)   TI MI   FA DO   DO FA (MI)

SO RE (DO)   RE SO   LA MI   MI LA (SO)

PERFECT 5th INTERVALS (Harmonic)

SO   LA   TI   DO   RE   MI
DO   RE   MI   FA   SO   LA

AUGMENTED 4TH/DIMINISHED 5th INTERVALS (Melodic)

FA TI (DO)   TI FA (MI)

AUGMENTED 4TH/DIMINISHED 5th INTERVALS (Harmonic)

TI   FA
FA   TI

(Key of D contd)

MAJOR 2nd INTERVALS (Melodic)

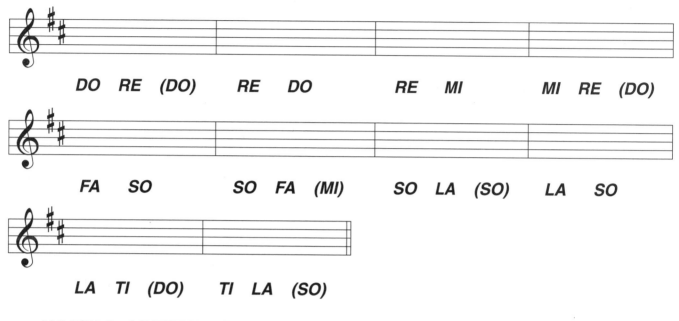

DO RE (DO)   RE DO   RE MI   MI RE (DO)

FA SO   SO FA (MI)   SO LA (SO)   LA SO

LA TI (DO)   TI LA (SO)

MAJOR 2nd INTERVALS (Harmonic)

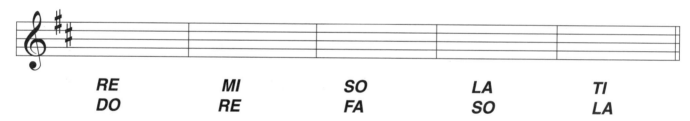

RE   MI   SO   LA   TI
DO   RE   FA   SO   LA

MINOR 7th INTERVALS (Melodic)

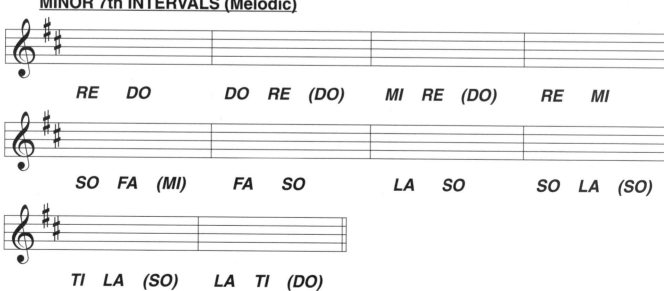

RE DO   DO RE (DO)   MI RE (DO)   RE MI

SO FA (MI)   FA SO   LA SO   SO LA (SO)

TI LA (SO)   LA TI (DO)

SUPPLEMENTARY WORKSHEETS

(Key of D contd)

MINOR 7th INTERVALS (Harmonic)

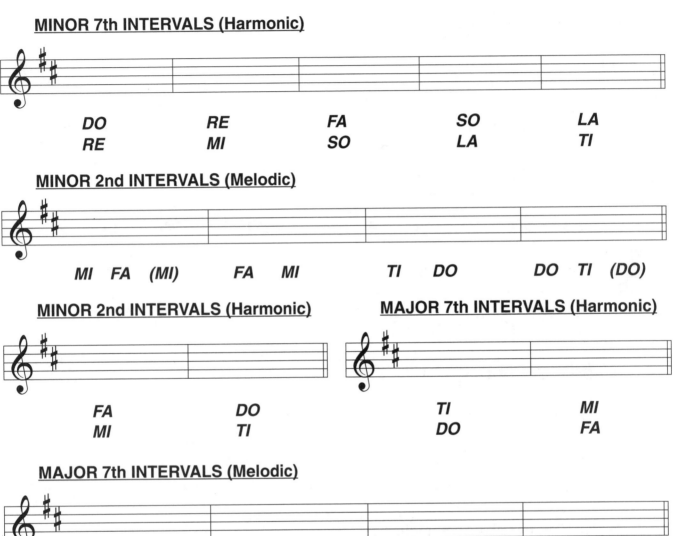

DO	RE	FA	SO	LA
RE	MI	SO	LA	TI

MINOR 2nd INTERVALS (Melodic)

MI FA (MI)   FA MI   TI DO   DO TI (DO)

MINOR 2nd INTERVALS (Harmonic)   MAJOR 7th INTERVALS (Harmonic)

FA	DO		TI	MI
MI	TI		DO	FA

MAJOR 7th INTERVALS (Melodic)

DO TI (DO)   TI DO   FA MI   MI FA (MI)

DIATONIC TRIADS

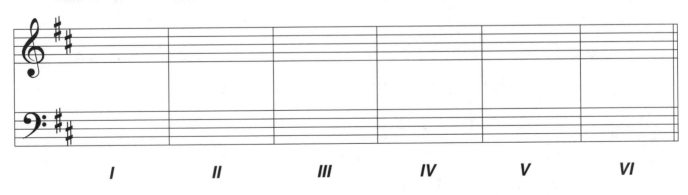

I	II	III	IV	V	VI

Supplementary Worksheets - Key of Bb

RESOLUTIONS

DO RE DO   DO FA MI   DO LA SO   DO TI DO

MAJOR 3rd INTERVALS (Melodic)

DO MI   MI DO   FA LA (SO)   LA FA (MI)

SO TI (DO)   TI SO

MAJOR 3rd INTERVALS (Harmonic)

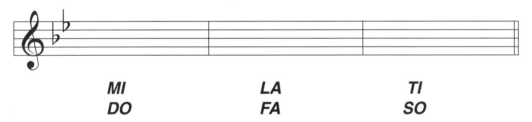

MI   LA   TI
DO   FA   SO

MINOR 6th INTERVALS (Melodic)

MI DO   DO MI   LA FA (MI)   FA LA (SO)

TI SO   SO TI (DO)

(Key of Bb contd)

MINOR 6th INTERVALS (Harmonic)

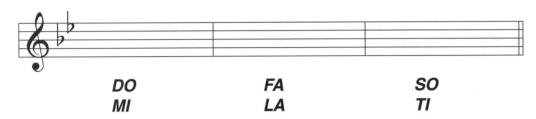

DO	FA	SO
MI	LA	TI

MINOR 3rd INTERVALS (Melodic)

RE FA (MI)   FA RE (DO)   MI SO   SO MI

LA DO   DO LA (SO)   RE TI (DO)   TI RE (DO)

MINOR 3rd INTERVALS (Harmonic)

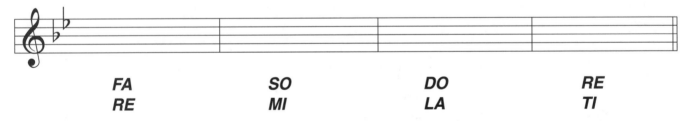

FA	SO	DO	RE
RE	MI	LA	TI

MAJOR 6th INTERVALS (Melodic)

DO LA (SO)   LA DO   RE TI (DO)   TI RE (DO)

FA RE (DO)   RE FA (MI)   SO MI   MI SO

218

(Key of Bb contd)

MAJOR 6th INTERVALS (Harmonic)

LA	TI	RE	MI
DO	RE	FA	SO

PERFECT 4th INTERVALS (Melodic)

DO FA (MI) FA DO   RE SO   SO RE (DO)

MI LA (SO) LA MI   SO DO   DO SO

LA RE (DO) RE LA (SO)   TI MI   MI TI (DO)

PERFECT 4th INTERVALS (Harmonic)

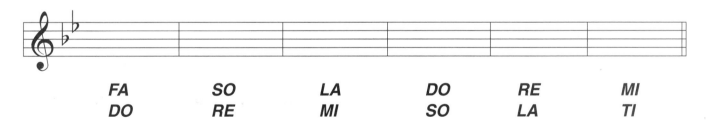

FA	SO	LA	DO	RE	MI
DO	RE	MI	SO	LA	TI

(Key of Bb contd)

PERFECT 5th INTERVALS (Melodic)

DO   SO   SO   DO   RE   LA   (SO)   LA   RE   (DO)

MI   TI   (DO)   TI   MI   FA   DO   DO   FA   (MI)

SO   RE   (DO)   RE   SO   LA   MI   MI   LA   (SO)

PERFECT 5th INTERVALS (Harmonic)

SO   LA   TI   DO   RE   MI
DO   RE   MI   FA   SO   LA

AUGMENTED 4TH/DIMINISHED 5th INTERVALS (Melodic)

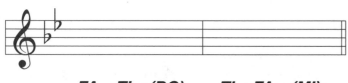

FA   TI   (DO)   TI   FA   (MI)

AUGMENTED 4TH/DIMINISHED 5th INTERVALS (Harmonic)

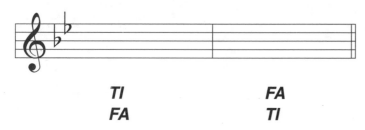

TI   FA
FA   TI

(Key of Bb contd)

MAJOR 2nd INTERVALS (Melodic)

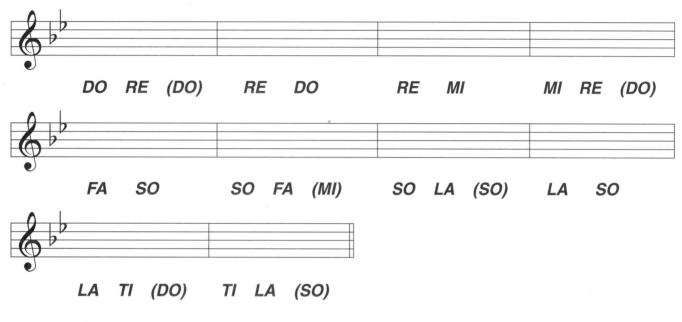

DO RE (DO)   RE DO   RE MI   MI RE (DO)

FA SO   SO FA (MI)   SO LA (SO)   LA SO

LA TI (DO)   TI LA (SO)

MAJOR 2nd INTERVALS (Harmonic)

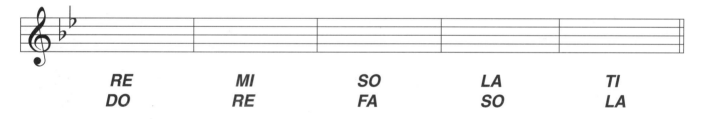

RE   MI   SO   LA   TI
DO   RE   FA   SO   LA

MINOR 7th INTERVALS (Melodic)

RE DO   DO RE (DO)   MI RE (DO)   RE MI

SO FA (MI)   FA SO   LA SO   SO LA (SO)

TI LA (SO)   LA TI (DO)

(Key of Bb contd)

MINOR 7th INTERVALS (Harmonic)

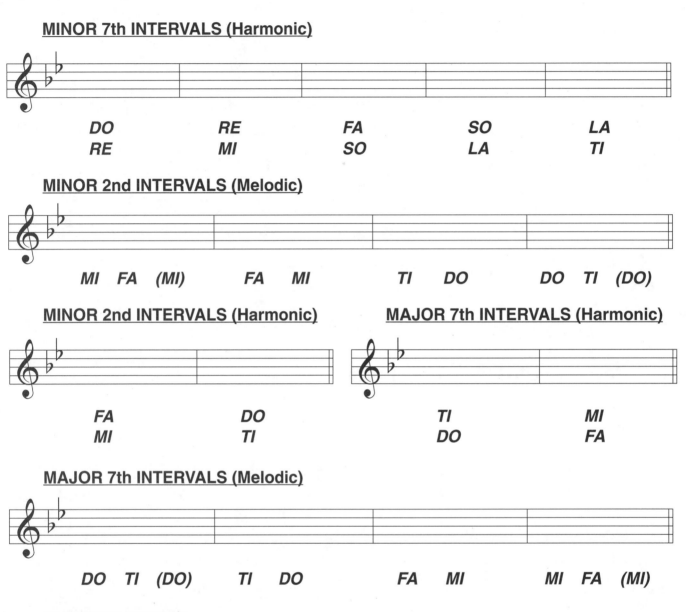

DIATONIC TRIADS

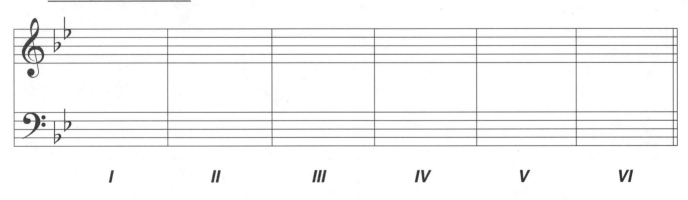